A QUESTION
OF ETHICS

A QUESTION OF ETHICS

Canadians Speak Out

Maureen Mancuso
(University of Guelph)

Michael M. Atkinson
(University of Saskatchewan)

André Blais
(Université de Montréal)

Ian Greene
(York University)

Neil Nevitte
(University of Toronto)

Toronto Oxford New York
Oxford University Press
1998

Oxford University Press
70 Wynford Drive, Don Mills, Ontario M3C 1J9
http://www.oupcan.com

Oxford New York
Athens Auckland Bangkok Bogotà Buenos Aires Calcutta
Cape Town Chennai Dar es Salaam Delhi Florence Hong Kong
Istanbul Karachi Kuala Lumpur Madrid Melbourne Mexico City
Mumbai Nairobi Paris São Paulo Singapore Taipei Tokyo
Toronto Warsaw

and associated companies in
Berlin Ibadan

Oxford is a trade mark of Oxford University Press

Canadian Cataloguing in Publication Data

Main entry under title:

A question of ethics : Canadians speak out

Includes bibliographical references and index.

ISBN 0-19-541353-9

1. Political ethics — Canada — Public opinion.   2. Political ethics —
Public opinion.   3. Public opinion — Canada.   I. Mancuso, Maureen.

JA79.Q47 1998   172   C98-931859-1

Cover & Text Design: Brett Miller

1 2 3 4 - 01 00 99 98

This book is printed on permanent (acid-free) paper ∞.

Printed in Canada

→ Table of Contents

→ List of Figures

➔ List of Tables

Studying political ethics can be a confusing pursuit. The very nature of politics dictates that those involved rarely mean exactly what they say, or say exactly what they mean. Everyone supports ideals like freedom and equality, but exactly how those principles are transformed into concrete policies is rarely clear. For that matter, it's often hard to tell just what 'lower taxes' means, if anything. In the realm of ethics, we all desire more honesty and more 'ethical' politics—no one prefers 'unethical' political behaviour—but what sorts of actions are more 'ethical' than others is not something that can be easily agreed upon or recognized. Personal standards vary: what some people might consider appropriate behaviour can be shocking to others. When those in public office overestimate the public's tolerance for some questionable form of activity, the result is a scandal. Some of this difference in interpretation can be managed through explicit regulations and restrictions. Still, at the end of the day, no matter what rules, guidelines, and procedures are followed, what ultimately matters in a democracy like Canada is whether and to what extent the conduct of politicians conforms to what those who put them in office are entitled to expect.

The question then becomes: what are those expectations? What does the Canadian public really think about political ethics? What sort of behaviour do they demand from their public officials, and what kinds of cut corners will they shrug off? This book is an attempt to tackle these questions head-on, by documenting and exploring the attitudes of individual Canadians on issues of political conduct. The results will be of interest to three different audiences. Students of political ethics will find the comprehensive empirical data about mass opinion useful. Those in public office themselves should finally have access to a clear indication of the standards they are expected to uphold. On the other hand, they will no longer be able to claim ignorance when they step on toes. Finally, and perhaps most notably, it can be a direct source of feedback to those who created it—the public. It is easy to find information in the media, in press releases, and in political speeches, about 'what people want'. We asked Canadians themselves what they want, and we hope that their answers are interesting.

We never could have listened so extensively and in such detail without the assistance and co-operation of many others. We are indebted to the Social Science and Humanities Research Council of Canada and the University of Guelph for their financial assistance. Louise Solda and the Development Office at the University of Guelph provided the facilities necessary for conducting the surveys. David Northrup from the Institute for Social Research at York University supplied the random sample and graciously led the training sessions for our student callers. Early and crucial direction was obtained from the participants in our Ethics Workshop held in Elora.

This project has provided an excellent learning opportunity for students at all our universities. Their enthusiasm, commitment, and professionalism made the data collection an enjoyable and rewarding experience. To them we owe much, and we thank them one and all: Scott Adnams, Azeeza Ali, Tricia Benn, Geneviève Bouchard, Seree Boulianne, John Burns, Karen Cameron, Catherine Canary, Donnalyn Charles, Paul Courville, Mary Cremer, Barbara Curran, Julie Demerchant, Nicole Dennison, Isabelle Dufour, Shanti Fernando, Wendy Finlay, Melissa Gabler, Mary-Jo Gordon, Iain Grant, Geneviève Grenier, Kim Groenendyk, Ryan Hunter, Jeff Johnstone, Georgina Kelly, Lucinda Kennedy, Carolyn Lefèbvre, Cory MacDonald, Patrik Marier, Gary Martin, Anne Marie Martin, Alex Moiseev, Erik

Monpetit, Aimé Murigande, Amanda Ng, Colleen Nichols, Hélène O'Hara, Easton Phidd, Crystal Ralph, Myleno Renauld, Yvon Sauvé, Jonathan Scott, Mary-Beth Tersigni, Kim Thalheimer, Cedrik Thérrien, Martin Turcotte, Marie-Claude Villeneuve, Richard Vollans, Karen Wilson, and Jamie Wingate. Gerald Bierling of McMaster University ably managed this stalwart group.

At the University of Guelph, Joanne Duncan-Robinson entered the data and provided much-appreciated technical assistance. Lorraine Black's administrative finesse kept the project on an even keel. William Christian supplied helpful comments both arch and insightful on the entire manuscript. Melissa Gabler, Tricia Benn, Lucinda Kennedy, Karen Wilson, Wendy Finlay, and Cassandra Pervin provided expert research assistance.

At Oxford University Press, Euan White and Ric Kitowski recognized the potential of this project immediately and helped shepherd it along. Phyllis Wilson and the rest of the editorial team assisted in refining the content and presentation of the material.

Finally, to the over 1,400 Canadians who took the time to participate in the survey, we thank you for your time and interest, and hope you can find a bit of yourselves somewhere in the pages that follow. Listen for your voice in the chorus of Canadians speaking out—let's hope our political leaders are also tuned in and paying attention.

Introduction

A QUESTION
OF ETHICS

In 1867 Canada was born as a new nation dedicated to promoting 'peace, order, and good government'. For about a hundred years we seem to have been fairly well satisfied with our performance. In the past 30, however, even though we seem to have held onto the first two ideals, there has been an ever-growing suspicion that the third is slipping away from us. The discovery of new depths in the public's cynicism about politicians and politics is no longer news. We don't seem to trust the people we elect to run our governments, and we vote for them only because the alternatives appear even worse. That is, if we bother to vote at all. Public participation in the political process continues to drop, reflecting growing dissatisfaction with the results.[1]

The political realm, conceived as a deliberative arena where decisions of great public consequence would be thoughtfully debated, seems to have become a farcical shouting match. Pre-choreographed arguments staged by a few party heavyweights who don't even believe their own scripts have squeezed out informed discussion. Our politicians resort to behaviour—pranks, lies, and vicious name-calling—that would not be tolerated in a school yard.

When politicians are in the news, what gets the headlines? Senators who take home $65,000 a year but never show up for work. The 'abolishing' of a tax by merely renaming it in a few provinces. MPs who hire each other's sons and daughters to work

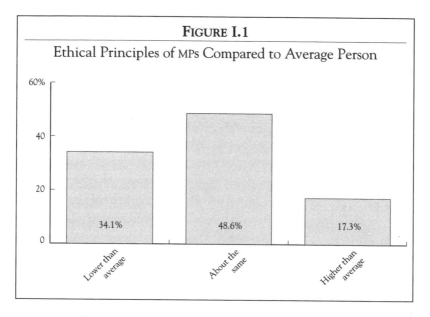

FIGURE I.1

Ethical Principles of MPs Compared to Average Person

in their offices. The Prime Minister 'rolls the dice' with the future of the country. We give a small group of individuals enormous power over our well-being, and they treat it as a game or a way to make money.

Of course, we tend to take the real accomplishments of the political process for granted. Have you talked to anyone in the States about medical bills lately? Canada's health care system, though it may not be perfect, represents a triumph of legislative will and foresight, and there are innumerable other services we rely on that are usually taken care of competently—in winter the roads are usually ploughed; children go to school; the elderly, the unemployed, and the poor are given financial assistance. Our governments may create new problems even as they solve others, but on the whole they do well enough that the United Nations consistently ranks Canada as one of the best (and often *the* best) countries to live in.[2]

Why then has it become commonplace to hear of a 'crisis of confidence' in our political leaders and institutions? Why did we

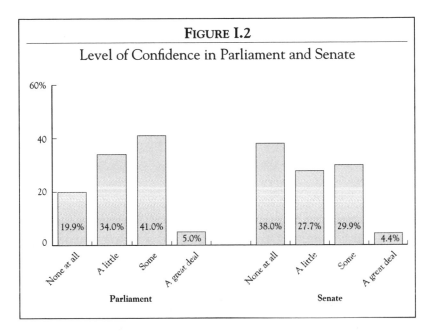

FIGURE I.2

Level of Confidence in Parliament and Senate

Parliament: None at all 19.9%, A little 34.0%, Some 41.0%, A great deal 5.0%

Senate: None at all 38.0%, A little 27.7%, Some 29.9%, A great deal 4.4%

find that a majority of Canadians we spoke to have little to no confidence in Parliament and that more than a third believe that MPs have lower than average ethical standards (Figure I.1)?[3] What accounts for the poor opinion people have of their political institutions (Figure I.2)? Is our political system fundamentally flawed, or does it just attract the wrong sort of leader? We want to be proud of our country and of the principles and behaviour of those we choose as public figures. We want their principles to reflect, and even improve upon, our own. We want them to be heroes, but they turn out to be no better than the guy down the street who we suspect cheats on his taxes.

A Question of Ethics?

To be sure, one force driving this cynicism is the bad publicity that politics attracts in the news media and the public consciousness. What draws our attention are the slip-ups, the scandals, the lapses in judgement, and the occasional downright illegalities. At the same time, are we sure that we are being fair to our elected representatives? Is what they consider a carefully crafted compromise quickly dismissed as a shameless betrayal? Maybe we don't fully understand all the complicated and difficult choices our officials have to make every day. It is a long way from peace, order, and good government to section 25, subsection 3, paragraph 2 of the third reading of a bill. Even politically sophisticated private citizens may not realize what has to go into the process of turning ideals into policy.

On the other hand, politicians do themselves no favours. If we don't fully understand them, they seem determined to misunderstand us, especially what types of political behaviour offend us. The disgraced official who insists, 'I did nothing I considered wrong' is a stock character in political theatre. Sometimes this naïveté is just a pose, but sometimes it is sincere. However much elected officials try to emphasize that they stay in touch with 'the folks back home', the reality is that most of their time is spent with other politicians or the associates of politicians—civil servants, lobbyists, journalists. Even the media sometimes have a hard time figuring out what is and is not acceptable to the general public: exaggerated stories of scandals are sometimes greeted with a yawn, or letters to the editor often complain that 'the real story' is being ignored.[4]

Canadians Speak Out

This book is primarily an attempt to confront these kinds of misunderstandings. Thus far the boundaries of political ethics in Canada have been determined largely by trial and error. The trouble is, all those errors and trials are costly both to the public interest and to public confidence in our political institutions. To try to map out more precisely the contours of acceptability in political behaviour, we went directly to the public by means of a broad-based survey. In a democracy, it is the 'ordinary' citizens who vote politicians into and out of power, and it is their 'ordinary' attitudes and opinions that determine those votes. We have tried to measure some of those attitudes, in the hope of understanding better why elections so often seem to be about 'voting against' rather than 'voting for'.

Opinions about politics come in many shapes and sizes, and much of politics is a process of combining and reconciling different opinions about what should be done with society's resources. We can't settle the left-wing-right-wing argument (an impossible task, despite what editorialists might say, and it doesn't help us much anyway when it comes to trust in government). But in the realm of political ethics everyone agrees right is preferable to wrong. What is disputed is what constitutes right behaviour. Since every political activity is blurred by qualifications and shades of grey, and since conflicts and choices are inherent in the political process, absolute moral purity is unattainable. Nor is it even desirable, for to some degree at least we expect our elected representatives to promote our interests even at the expense of someone else's.

We need to know the actual operative ethical standards in force among the Canadian public. Just how harshly do Canadians judge the ethical conduct of their elected officials? Politicians need this information in order to adapt their behaviour to the expectations of the electorate. The media need it not only so that they can align their coverage to give their readers what they want, but so that they can help educate them as well. Academics (like us) need this information so that we can better understand how and why the public feels as it does. And the public needs to know because these attitudes fundamentally shape our shared political culture. Of course, the public view is not a single, indivisible entity, but consists of millions of diverse individual opinions. Differences of opinion may just be quirks or they may reflect deep and essential variations in experience and outlook. What is acceptable to one group may provoke the ire of another. We need to understand this diversity and how it affects political practice. Finally, we need this information because you need to understand a situation before you have any chance of improving it. The cries for political reform are strong and loud, but until we know just what is broken we may end up 'fixing' the wrong parts of the political machinery.

What to Listen For

This book attempts to fill some of these gaps in Canada's ethical self-understanding. Chapter 1 discusses the basic concepts and principles of political ethics. The apportionment and use of power in democratic societies is affected by both theoretical and practical constraints. We give an overview of how ethical considerations arise out of and feed back into these ideals and functional patterns. Moreover, our particular democratic society has developed its own specific brand of ethical interpretation and regulation. We begin by discussing the ethical rules, such as they are, that apply to public officials in Canada.

Chapter 2 expands on this background and lays out the methodological and analytical framework that guides the rest of the book. Readers who are not particularly interested in such matters can skim this chapter and still keep pace with the results in those that follow. For those who stay with us, we explore further the importance of public attitudes in gauging the ethical temperature of a situation, and present in detail the instrument used to probe these attitudes. We document the design and execution of the survey of over 1,400 Canadians that is the heart of this study (the questionnaire itself is reproduced in the Appendix). What emerges from the answers we collected is a reliable impression of what Canadians in general think about issues of political ethics. This chapter provides a basis for assessing and understanding our results.

Each of the next four chapters examines in detail a particular type of problematic political behaviour. Our survey asked respondents to assess a large number of hypothetical situations, which could be grouped into four basic kinds of activity. In Chapter 3 we jump right into the murky waters of 'conflict of interest', a term more often tossed about than understood, and used to cover a wide range of ethically questionable activity. Chapter 4 examines 'gifts and gains', that is, the perks and special privileges that seem to be so common in political life. The grand old game of rewarding your friends and supporters (and punishing your enemies) with governmental largesse and influence is the topic of Chapter 5, 'patronage'. And Chapter 6 covers lying, an apparently fundamental option of politicians.

In turn, we look at each type of behaviour in several ways. We discuss examples of the behaviours, the forces that pressure officials to indulge in or avoid them, and the arguments that have been made to defend or rationalize their use. The analysis of the survey data shows how well such arguments play on the stage of public opinion. We detail the specifics of each type of activity—how the circumstances of an activity produce gradations in its acceptability and to what extent the conventional wisdom about the public standards is correct. We also explore how different segments of the population vary in their opinions of each type of behaviour, and look for the 'fault lines'—demarcations between segments of the population who hold differing views.

What will emerge from these discussions and some concluding thoughts is a better understanding of how our fellow Canadians feel about political ethics and how those feelings apply in specific cases. We hope this new map of ethical standards will provoke more public and political discussion: are these standards appropriate, realistic, and consistent? Are we being unfair to politicians by condemning them for what we ourselves would do in private life? Or perhaps this is not a contradiction at all if public life is seen as a higher calling that requires higher standards. Are the standards we express in our opinions truly the standards we aspire to in our more contemplative and philosophical moments? Do we want the unattainable, or are we settling for less than we deserve?

Ultimately, we hope that hearing what their fellow Canadians have to say will give readers more insight into our political processes and culture. Much as we'd like to, we cannot require public officials to buy this book, but we can suggest that a concerted effort to listen to what the country is saying would be profitable. Today, with cynicism and public frustration on the rise, the abilities and performance of political institutions and players are loudly called into question—not just in ideological arguments about how big government should be, but also in attacks on the very legitimacy of our system as a properly functioning democracy. In such an environment we need to ensure that when Canadians speak out they are heard, understood, and ultimately heeded.

✦

Chapter One

POLITICAL ETHICS IN CANADA—
THEORY AND PRACTICE

✦

SCENES FROM THE CANADIAN EXPERIENCE

In December 1996, Prime Minister Jean Chrétien suffered a serious blow to his credibility when he claimed on CBC Television's national 'town hall' session that he had never promised to abolish the Goods and Services Tax (GST). In fact, the Liberal Party's 1993 election platform, known as the Red Book, promised that the GST would be replaced, and many Liberal candidates, including Chrétien himself, referred to this as a commitment to abolish the GST. Sheila Copps, who became deputy Prime Minister, was so categorical about this issue that she had promised to resign if the GST was not repealed. Although she made light of this promise for a time, a storm of controversy eventually forced her to resign and contest a by-election in early 1996. And Liberal MP John Nunziata was expelled from the Liberal caucus because he had voted against a Liberal budget that he thought broke the GST promise. His stance was in part validated when he was re-elected in 1997 as an Independent member.

Clearly Chrétien would not have taken such a firm position that harmonizing the GST with provincial sales taxes is an acceptable method of 'replacing' the GST unless he believed that he was ethically above reproach. After all, in the introduction to the Liberal party's 1996 evaluation of its three-year performance, 'A Record of Achievement', Chrétien wrote, 'of all the Red Book commitments we have kept, none gives me greater pride than our living up to our pledge to govern with integrity. . . . We have been honest with Canadians.' But the polls indicated that most Canadians did not think that it was honest to equate tax harmonization with the promise to replace the GST, and a week after the town hall debacle, Chrétien had the political sense to apologize for having possibly left the wrong impression about the Liberal's plans for the GST.[1] By the following spring, it was clear that the voters were still displeased with the Liberals' interpretation of their promise, but not upset enough to remove them from power in the general election.[2]

Also in December 1996, Alberta's ethics commissioner, Robert Clark, for a second time cleared Premier Ralph Klein of any wrongdoing in the Multi-Corp affair. In late 1993, the president of Multi-Corp had sold Mrs Klein 10,000 shares of the company at nearly 40 per cent below market value and told her she didn't need to pay for the shares until she sold them. Several of Klein's closest aides or their spouses received similar deals. At the time, Multi-Corp was doing business in east Asia, where the endorsement of the corporation by the Alberta government would be a valuable business asset. In fact, Ralph Klein travelled to east Asia in 1994, although the ethics commissioner in a cursory investigation could find no evidence that he had promoted Multi-Corp.

But the fact that his wife had received a special deal on the Multi-Corp shares that wasn't available to all Albertans and the fact that he himself was in a position to enhance the value of these shares had placed Ralph Klein in an ethically challenging situation: he had the opportunity to advance his own private interests through his elected office. Clark blamed himself for the Kleins' mistake in accepting the shares because he said he had not questioned them carefully enough at the time. But is this really an appropriate model for public service: do what you want, unless someone happens to notice and call you on it? Maybe so: Klein's popularity ratings remained high even as the affair was revealed in the media.

Klein and Chrétien came under fire for apparent breaches of ethics, but so far they appear to have avoided long-term damage. This may be because the public accepts what they did as proper behaviour. On the other hand, perhaps the public is not entirely clear as to what was actually done or has been confused by the prescriptions of the various 'spin doctors' that have offered their opinions. Perhaps the public clearly disapproves of such behaviour, but this disapproval is outweighed by its satisfaction with other aspects of these politicians' performances. There are many factors that complicate any effort to measure just what is and is not palatable to the public's ethical taste. Indeed, that taste may not even be consistent—perhaps politicians are criticized publicly for behaviour that private citizens would never be questioned about. Making ethical determinations is a tricky business, and in the political realm, doubly so.

Of course, sometimes it's easy to tell that things are amiss: from 1987 to 1991, a number of Saskatchewan Conservative MLAs submitted fictitious expense claims from imaginary companies against a pooled account of their communications allowances. They then handed out the money (often in wads of $1,000-dollar bills) to each other for various personal treats ranging from home computers to a fancy engraved riding saddle to a Hawaiian holiday. So far, 19 MLAs have been charged—and at least 10 convicted—of various degrees of involvement in a scheme that directly defrauded the public of more than $800,000. In 1988, MP Michel Gravel admitted to taking some $100,000 in kickbacks and bribes in his capacity as member responsible for government contracts in Hull. In 1994, the newly elected Liberals expelled MP Jag Bhaduria from the party when it came to light that he had falsified his résumé, listing academic degrees and qualifications he had never obtained.

Scandals like these—their frequency and almost clockwork regularity—have to an extent desensitized the public to such revelations. At what point does the public reaction change from

'What an outrage!' to 'So what else is new?' Countless observers have noted the increasing public cynicism about politics and politicians in Canada.[3] This is a problem not just for politicians, even the best of whom must defend themselves against a perception that they are crooks and liars, but also for society as a whole. Ultimately, if the people lose faith in their political system, they tend to withdraw from politics altogether: they stop making the effort to stay informed, take positions, or even vote. Democracy does not work well if the people stop caring.

Other situations are not so easy to judge. When John Turner let stand a slew of last-minute patronage appointments made by Pierre Trudeau on his way out of office, was he honouring a commitment, or did he, as Brian Mulroney claimed, 'have a choice' and simply choose to serve his cronies instead of Canada? For that matter, when Mulroney invoked an obscure constitutional clause six years later to pack the Senate with extra Conservative appointees in order to pass the GST, was he upholding the primacy of the elected House over the appointed Senate, or simply riding roughshod over informed dissent? Alberta Premier Don Getty, arguably in effective control of much of Canada's oil and gas industry, speculated extensively in oil and gas stocks: criminal, or just unwise? Who was more in the wrong over the 1993–4 Pearson airport affair—the Conservatives who, on the eve of an election, approved a contract to privatize the airport that was phenomenally lucrative for their supporters, or the Liberals, who tore up the signed contracts and tried to avoid paying compensation? When Ontario MPP Peter Kormos appeared as a (fully clothed) tabloid pin-up boy, was it a clever publicity stunt or a clear debasement of the dignity of public office?

It is obvious that there is some sort of 'ethical gap' between how politicians and the public interpret certain situations. We can presume that most politicians are not intentionally trying to annoy the voters—and yet they regularly do so by misjudging what the public will tolerate. In the broad arena of policy issues, this is what politics is all about: success goes to those who are astute enough to discern what the people want and how much of what they don't want they will put up with. In ethical terms, however, mistakes in judging public opinion are essentially failures to understand the fundamental contract between office holders and voters. When we elect someone, we do so with an expectation that he or she will adhere to certain standards of conduct and probity. What makes it difficult for the official is that these standards are by no means explicit and clear; rather they consist of attitudes and opinions that are hard to pinpoint. Some of these have solidified into actual rules of behaviour, but many are more on the level of common-sense etiquette. We have the same structure in society as a whole: how one should behave is governed by formal rules (laws) and informal norms (courtesy).

POLITICAL ETHICS IN A DEMOCRATIC SYSTEM

If we are to understand how ethical judgements are made and why politicians make particular ones that sometimes go so spectacularly wrong, we need to understand where these standards of behaviour come from. Ultimately, they are the expression of basic moral and political principles. In the rest of this chapter, we will discuss these principles and the environment of ideals in which they operate. This will also allow us to examine how they are reflected and occasionally distorted in the various rules and guidelines that have developed to govern the activities of those in public office.

Rules and Expectations

In fact, the most fundamental democratic principle is that governments should express the wishes of the people. We have set up a large variety of institutions that help to translate those wishes—

millions of individual sets of assorted priorities, opinions, and preferences—into more or less coherent public policy. Elections, legislatures, political parties, interest groups, polls, press conferences, and even constitutions all serve in this admittedly imperfect process. Ultimately, however, we really have only two ways of keeping this process on track, and making sure that those involved are working for the system, and not for themselves. We make rules to outlaw or punish the type of behaviour that is unacceptable, and we express preferences about what sort of behaviour is desired.

In the realm of ethics, we have formal restrictions—the written rules and guidelines—and informal boundaries—the attitudes and expectations about what is proper or improper. These two sources of evaluation do not necessarily coincide. Just as it is possible to be considered a rotten person even without breaking any of the Ten Commandments, a politician can follow all the applicable rules and still offend our expectations of ethical behaviour. The rules refer to a minimal number of absolutely unacceptable acts, but in the ethical realm, we expect more than just minimally acceptable behaviour.

The rules are few in number because ultimately they are an expression of what is considered out of bounds by society as a whole. Only the most obvious or glaring improprieties can generate hard and fast rules, because different people have different opinions of what is proper. This is, of course, why we have a government and a political system: we all do not agree on everything. Almost everyone condemns taking bribes: thus bribery is against the law, and politicians who indulge in it have been sent to jail. But harmonizing a tax rather than replacing it is not so obviously a crime. Not everyone would criminalize lucky investors who are in the right place at the right time. Our evaluations of these activities must eventually rest, not on clear and well-defined rules, but on vague and hard-to-measure notions like attitudes, opinions, and beliefs. In a court of law, what matters is the letter of the law; in the court of public opinion, what matters is the spirit.

Rules and expectations are the expressions of personal and social standards, but these standards evolve from more fundamental considerations. Some of them, like the golden rule, are universal, in that they do not apply only to the political world. Others, though, are specific to politics, because politics brings with it a number of complicating factors.

Roles and Interests

A fundamental aspect of democracy is that members of the government are drawn from the ranks of the governed: rules apply equally to the rulers as well as the ruled. Paradoxically, this means that public officials are still fundamentally different from everyone else because they are both public and private citizens. Once they are elevated to office, they add to their ordinary rights and duties an extensive set of additional privileges and responsibilities. They gain a public life that overlays their private life and can interfere with it. In particular they still have their own bank accounts to manage, but unlike the rest of us, they also share some direct control over the public purse. What happens when these public and private interests come into conflict?

Even in the private realm, problems arise because people perform multiple roles. Busy people with complicated lives are particularly vulnerable. When you hear people say that they are going to take off one hat and put on another, or that for these purposes they are wearing this or that hat, then you realize that role conflicts are a common problem and that people have learned to deal with them in a routine manner. This is not to minimize their importance, only to recognize that such entanglements are hard to avoid in the modern world.

Politics complicates things further, because an elected official has to manage an assortment of private roles, as well as a public persona that is multi-faceted and divided into separate and potentially competing roles. An MP has obligations to his constituency as a representative, and to the whole country as a legislator. He is also a member of a party organization in which he has further duties. A woman MP, simply because there are so few of them, will undoubtedly feel obliged to act as a spokesperson for all women; she will certainly be seen as one no matter what she does. The same holds true for politicians who belong to any minority group. What happens when these various roles clash—when what's good for the riding isn't quite what's best for the country?

This mixture of roles and interests can be, and usually is, confusing for public officials, especially newly elected ones. After every change of government there is usually a rash of 'oops' problems, as newly anointed legislators find themselves wearing the wrong hat to the wrong occasion—the first year or so of Brian Mulroney's accident-prone first cabinet and Bob Rae's 'we can't believe we won' Ontario government are particularly good examples. A private person may also wear many hats: wife, mother, employee, daughter, and maybe softball coach. Conflicts between these roles can be a source of great personal and family stress, but it doesn't affect the general public. However, when an MP makes a bad choice among roles, public money is spent inefficiently or public resources are wasted. The continuing coincidence of impressive government facilities just happening to locate themselves within the sitting PM's riding is a possible example.

There are few guidelines for resolving conflicts of roles and interests, and many politicians involved in scandals have tried to claim ignorance or have complained that they just needed help to keep from inadvertently straying off the path. Again, the most obvious breaches are prohibited by laws and rules, but before a legal line is crossed, politicians are allowed a great deal of latitude. They are forced to rely on their own discretion in many areas. This means that citizens also must rely on their discretion and hope that it is used responsibly and impartially.

PRINCIPLES OF ASPIRATION

What guides the exercise of discretionary judgement in ethically charged situations? The answer is hardly clear, and it varies from person to person. In some cases, it appears that the basic principle of motivation is nothing but greed. Luckily this is not always the case. There are some common themes that emerge from political discussions—academic, popular, and professional—that describe basic principles of aspiration. These principles encapsulate the concerns which, in an ideal world, a perfect politician would always hold at the forefront of his or her mind when making public decisions.

One notion that almost always eludes exact definition is the 'public interest'. Moreover, one duty of political leaders is to help give shape to this concept: laws and policies should promote the public interest; corruption is often defined as behaviour that harms it. The daily battle between Government and Opposition, when it is about anything, is basically about whose definition of the public interest should hold sway. Nevertheless, the notion that somewhere out there is an ideal, if perhaps indescribable, public interest is basic to our notion of politics.

It follows that in a representative democracy, because each of us cannot directly pursue the public interest, we expect that those we elect to act on our behalf will serve as responsible trustees of our interest. We delegate to them some of our authority over our own lives, with the understanding that they will combine a respect for our continually expressed wishes with their own good judgement.

Elected officials have a responsibility of fiduciary trust, that is, a moral and ethical obligation, to promote and implement democratic principles, and if there is a conflict between their self-interest and the public responsibility, the duty of public trust comes first. Similarly, they are expected to behave impartially and fairly and to be accountable for their public actions. One of the time-honoured tools for promoting these principles is the rule of law, the concept that public policy is furthered through laws sanctioned by the democratic process. These laws must apply equally to everyone (unless there is a compelling reason for unequal treatment) and must be administered and adjudicated as impartially as possible.

The key to achieving impartiality is for officials to maintain their sense of autonomy, or independence from inappropriate influences on their decisions. If an official is beholden to some private interest, how can we expect him to decide in favour of the public interest when push comes to shove? This is a particularly tricky principle, since we don't really want completely autonomous politicians, who are sometimes called 'loose cannons'. They should serve the public interest, and at the same time do largely as we say. When we suspect that a politician serves another master, such as a campaign contributor, autonomy is compromised. When a politician gives a favour in return for that contribution, autonomy is shattered, along with the public trust. In other words, an elected official must maintain autonomy against the influence not only of external actors in the political pageant, but also of his own personal interests.

PRINCIPLES OF OPERATION

Autonomy is difficult for a politician to maintain partly because politics is not simply an abstract system, operating in a vacuum. The ideals we seek to fulfil must play themselves out in a hands-on, sometimes dirty, sometimes ugly, arena of real-world constraints. It is said that those who wish to enjoy either sausages or laws should never watch either being made. Legislatures are made up of fallible, selfish, and occasionally foolish human beings, not selfless, altruistic angels. This means that the political ideals of representation and the public interest are twisted, bent, and processed by a series of imperfect institutions and arrangements, and we must take these principles of operation into account. On the other hand, it also makes politics a lot more fun to watch.

One institution that modifies how political ideals express themselves is the political party. Political parties, which are entirely the product of custom and tradition (few democratic constitutions make mention of parties), serve the noble purpose of aggregating the opinions of many like-minded citizens and transmitting them to a few powerful representatives.[4] But they do so by methods that are not so far removed from those of the street gang or crime family: cronyism, patron-client relationships, institutionalized hierarchies of influence, and single-minded reflexive opposition to any obstacles to their power. Party discipline, which is particularly strict in Canada compared to the United States and even Great Britain, requires MPs essentially to give up all control over their individual vote in the House of Commons. This is a serious compromise of an MP's autonomy: MPs are strongly beholden to the party that helps them get elected, and rare indeed is the MP who can survive voting against the party line.

A party's tentacles of influence also extend far out into society. Private citizens join parties not only to support causes they believe in, but also in expectation of reward and preferment once 'our guys' gain power. Parties provide to democracy a formalized network of accountability and responsibility—when the party in power makes a serious mistake, the entire party suffers the consequences, and so there is a powerful incentive not to anger the public. But this same network also transmits obligations and indebtedness that can foster all sorts of abuse. Members of a party are easily tempted to serve the party rather than the country; after all, the country can't get them a cushy job.

Then again, at times it can seem as though there is little difference between the various parties, since no matter who's on top, they still act the same way. There is a powerful sense of cohesion among politicians and especially legislators. They share a large number of rather exclusive experiences: in effect they all belong to the same club. And since this club makes the rules for everyone, it remains strongly in favour of policing its own members with no interference from anyone else. There is a suspicion on the part of legislators that no one 'outside' really understands what they go through, and in part this is correct. But this insularity and collegiality can be invoked to protect the legislature and members who have apparently misbehaved from outside scrutiny or punishment. Legislatures must have a high degree of autonomy at the institutional level if they are to make the hard choices that are often required in government. But this institutional autonomy also has a dark side, in that legislatures and legislators can too easily see themselves as above the law or beyond the reach of ordinary ethical restrictions. In fact, most long-lived Canadian governments—the Trudeau Liberals and the Mulroney Conservatives are only the most recent examples—have been accused of displaying this arrogance of power.

In such situations, the news media often claim to be the public's saviour: a public-spirited group interested only in truth and openness in government and in holding politicians' feet to the fire when they try to evade the issues. But news organizations, like political systems, are composed of high ideals and not so high practices. Sometimes the need for a compelling story outweighs the true significance of a news item, and so a minor misstep becomes a 'fiasco'. At other times, a serious error in government may be downplayed into a 'kerfuffle' if it is inconveniently timed or too difficult to explain in an allotted sound bite. Most news organizations are profit-making enterprises, each with its own agendas and biases that can affect its delivery of supposedly unbiased 'news'. Although journalists are vital participants in the game of political ethics, like politicians, they have private interests that may conflict with their duty to the 'public's right to know'.

Finally, there is simply the problem of rotten apples in the barrel. Recently it has become fashionable to trace many of the reported ethical lapses to a crisis in character—a deficiency in moral fibre that only seems to be worsening. Of course the question then becomes whether we are electing more scoundrels these days, or whether our political system helps to corrupt those drawn into it. Does it teach Dr Jekyll how to become the Honourable Mr Hyde? Any political system has to allow its officials to use discretionary judgement, but when that judgement is used in the service of personal greed rather than the public good, we can only hope that the system has reasonably effective means of limiting the damage and identifying and punishing the offenders.

REGULATING POLITICAL ETHICS IN CANADA

Principles of aspiration and operation, like those we've discussed, lead to specific but mostly unwritten expectations about behaviour. A common rule of thumb, often repeated by Canadian premiers and prime ministers to their ministers and members, is not to do anything that they would be embarrassed to see printed on the front page of their local newspaper. The problem with this approach, however, is that different politicians have different standards of embarrassment. Over the past few decades, largely in response to scandals instigated by apparently shameless politicians, Canadian governments have developed more detailed written ethics regulations.

One difficulty with trying to comprehend 'the rules' in Canada is that despite some broad similarities, each province and territory has its own idea of what those rules should be, and the federal government has yet another version. Each government adds its own twists, strengths, and loopholes, and each borrows from the others to a certain extent—in just the sort of experimental atmosphere that Canada's federal system encourages. If there is an overall pattern, it is that the federal regulations are less well developed. As in many other policy areas such as health care, much of the initiative in codifying ethical rules has come from the provinces. Federal action has tended to lag behind.

One of the most visible components of the growing regulatory regime has been the establishment of officers responsible for administering and interpreting ethics rules and guidelines. Ontario created the first, its integrity commissioner, in 1988. British Columbia followed suit with a conflict of interest commissioner in 1990, and most other provinces and territories have set up independent 'ethics czars', or at least small legislative commissions with similar responsibilities. Though these czars are not entirely independent of the governments they watch over, for the most part they report to the legislature itself. In other words, they are like the various Speakers in that they are expected to serve impartially the legislative process itself, and not the partisan machinery of government. The federal government appointed an ethics counsellor after the 1993 general election as part of the Chrétien Liberals' emphasis on integrity, but unlike his provincial counterparts, this czar reports directly to the Prime Minister.[5]

While some of the ethics czars have made the headlines in connection with investigations into charges of corruption or misconduct, most of their work and their impact has not been in ferreting out misbehaviour but, rather, in providing expert advice and guidance to politicians who are trying to do the right thing. In the past, even well-intentioned officials may have found themselves slipping into trouble simply because they had misinterpreted the restrictions or unintentionally made 'an error in judgement'. Now, not only do officials have someone to make those judgements for them, but they also have an obligation to consult the local expert, and thus less latitude to claim ignorance if they get ensnared in scandal. The Ontario integrity commissioner, Gregory Evans, for example, had received over 800 inquiries from members by 1997 and had issued a series of reports summarizing his rulings on problem areas and frequently asked questions.

One of the biggest areas of confusion in these inquiries was the handling of gifts. In his 1990–1 report, Evans considered the case of an MPP who was asked to attend the opening of a mine in his constituency. The MPP was offered a free airline ticket valued at $600. Because the event was in the riding, Evans deemed that it would not be improper to accept this gift, although it would have to be publicly disclosed. In a sense this gift helped an MPP perform his official responsibilities. On the other hand, an MPP who was offered a complimentary membership in a local yacht club was warned that if he accepted such a gift he would be in violation of the *Integrity Act*. Even though the club was a business located in the constituency, there was no public purpose, and significant private benefit, to be derived from accepting.[6] These are the sorts of fine determinations that Evans and his counterparts regularly confront. We can speculate about whether the MPPs involved would have been so careful if they had not been able to consult an ethics adviser.

OTTAWA—THE LOWEST COMMON DENOMINATOR

A whole chapter could be devoted to how each jurisdiction handles varying types of ethically sensitive activity. Since the federal regulatory scheme is in most ways the least well-developed, however, we will concentrate on Ottawa in particular. In other words, although the provincial governments are far from perfect, the biggest, most expensive government we support is also the most vulnerable.

One important distinction that should be kept in mind is the source of ethical rules. Some rules are found in the Criminal Code, which declares certain practices, such as bribery, to be illegal. Other rules stem from Acts of Parliament—legislation which is not part of the Criminal Code, but which nevertheless restricts certain types of activity. For example, the *Parliament of Canada Act* specifically forbids Members of Parliament from entering into contracts with the government. Finally, rules may arise from parliamentary Standing Orders, the set of internal rules of behaviour for MPs that extends from how to address the Speaker and other members to when a member must disclose a financial interest. In general, Criminal Code rules are the most specific, but very few unethical activities have actually been deemed illegal; the Standing Orders cover the broadest range of restrictions but are the least clear and least directly enforceable.

Because of this structure, the rules that apply in any situation are not part of some single, coherent whole: Standing Orders may overlap and adjust the interpretation of statutory provisions. The problem isn't so much that one contradicts the other outright, but that it is difficult to determine which is more relevant and applicable in any particular case. Though there is often no clear and unequivocal answer, one of the main activities of the various ethics czars is to craft well-considered opinions.

In fact, 'the Rules' are not so much a consistent set of restrictions, as a crazy quilt of regulations patched together over the years, usually in response to particular scandals or issues. The rules governing the awarding of government contracts (and thus incidentally touching on the area of 'kickbacks') date from the nineteenth century. Specific guidelines for cabinet ministers on conflict of interest first appeared in 1964, when Prime Minister Lester Pearson wrote to his ministers insisting that just obeying the letter of the law was insufficient. It was equally important to avoid the appearance of impropriety.[7] In 1973, Allan MacEachen, as President of the Privy Council, revisited these admonitions in a Green Paper that called for a legislated approach to the regulation of politicians' behaviour. The recommended legislation was shelved, however, in favour of another, more specific letter from the Prime Minister.

In 1986, Prime Minister Mulroney extended and widened the scope of these letters, producing a conflict-of-interest code for public office holders.[8] Although it did not have the force of law, this code detailed proper procedures for the handling of assets and treatment of special favours. Within a few months, 14 cabinet ministers or aides had run afoul of these guidelines, including Sinclair Stevens, whose transgressions resulted in a judicial inquiry. And the guidelines themselves were quickly modified when it appeared that the Prime Minister himself was in violation for having accepted a loan from the Progressive Conservative Party of Canada. Again, legislation to back up and codify the informal rules was called for, and again it never materialized.

The same process has essentially repeated itself several times since, and there is still no specific legislation governing conflict of interest in Parliament.[9] The only major innovation of the last decade has been the creation of the position of federal Ethics Counsellor. In general there is little enthusiasm in Parliament for new rules to restrict the activities of parliamentarians. Suggestions for reform have been made in reaction to particular scandals, but there is no real desire for change based on the expression of basic ethical principles. In fact, until recently, none of the various letters or guidelines even attempted to define what was meant by conflict of interest.

So it is not surprising that the rules are full of loopholes. Gifts that don't actually constitute bribery are effectively unrestricted—this includes gifts from parties to officials, and many forms of hospitality. Nothing but honour prevents members from using official influence or confidential information to further their private interests. Free foreign travel paid for by third parties is largely unregulated, although MPs (but not Senators) must declare such trips. Honoraria or fees for speaking engagements can be accepted without limit and without declaration. And the whole issue of lobbying remains a murky swamp.

The current system provides little in the way of transparency. The Standing Orders exhort members to declare when they have a private interest in a matter before the House. But without sifting through Hansard every day, it is almost impossible to discern whether members are carefully separating their public and private roles. In Britain and Australia, by comparison, interest declarations are collected annually and published for all to see. Members must detail their personal holdings and their assets, investments, gifts received, trips taken, and other sources of income (in Britain many MPs also have other employment in addition to their legislative responsibilities).[10] Sources of potential bias are thus matters of public record. There is no such comprehensive *Register of Members' Interests* in Canada. Though some special-purpose registers do exist, like the one covering MPs' sponsored foreign travel, even these are for internal use only. In most countries, notably the United States, rules on declaration extend to the spouses and dependent children of the elected official. A congressman can't hide his assets by keeping them in his wife's name. In Canada this extension was attempted briefly under Joe Clark in 1979 but was subsequently abandoned in the face of heated opposition from the Parliamentary Spouses Association.[11]

When allegations or rumours arise, each is dealt with on an *ad hoc*, case-by-case basis. There is no standing investigative procedure and no body responsible for looking into charges. The new Ethics Counsellor is at least a source of advice and guidance, but as we've noted, the office is hampered by its lack of autonomy. As a creature of the Prime Minister, the counsellor cannot inspire the same confidence as his more independent provincial counterparts. And not only does a weak investigative structure mean that wrongdoers can escape sanction, but it also deprives members of a way to clear their names when sullied by groundless accusations. Studies have shown that representatives want to do the right thing and that they struggle with the dilemmas inherent in legislative life.[12] More specific rules, backed by formalized mechanisms for addressing breaches, would help them to resolve and avoid these dilemmas.

Some political parties, notably Reform in 1993, have recognized this need and have tried to devise codes of conduct for their own members. Unfortunately, these codes are not just ethical codes of conduct but also prescriptions of political philosophy. Moreover, it quickly became evident that Reform's internal code was intended primarily as a partisan weapon to wield against rivals: by renouncing official perks, they planned to emphasize by contrast the apparent greediness of their opponents. The ploy backfired when a number of Reformers were found to have violated their own code before it could be used in an election.

Finally, lurking at the bottom, as a sort of catch-all is the rule that there must be a general election at least every five years. Formally known as 'electoral retribution', this rule states that even though politicians may follow all the official rules, if they offend the public too far, they will find themselves eventually out of work. In some ways this is the most important rule, because the fear of losing power is the ultimate motivator in a world that depends on self-policing. Often, however, this rule has been used to rationalize the lack of more specific rules, on the theory that legislating behaviour is too restrictive, and the people should be given the final say. The problem is that the chance to cast a ballot two or three times every decade doesn't really allow the voters much opportunity to fine-tune their opinions and preferences.

CONCLUSION

In a direct democracy, full of referenda and plebiscites, extensive rules for official behaviour are not needed because the public will is expressed frequently and in great detail. If an elected official does a poor job or subverts the public interest in favour of his own, he can be removed quickly. But citizens of a modern representative democracy like Canada must express their will through layers of government that dull the edge of public scrutiny. A contemporary parliament must be to some extent self-governing—not in the sense that it is answerable to no one, but rather in that it must be able to control its own behaviour adequately to ensure that it remains a reflection of the public will. The self-interest of parliamentarians must be secondary to the public interest. This ideal is easy to state and is uncontroversial; but to achieve it in the real world is more difficult. The record shows that Canada has taken some steps toward regulating obvious misbehaviour. The significant point, which is explored in the following pages, is that most political activity takes place in a large grey zone, where acceptability is a matter of degree and where appearance reigns supreme. Differences in perception can lead to raucous scandals. Role overlap becomes role confusion, which becomes role interference.

How then can we make ethical determinations in a complex democracy like Canada? It is not enough to look solely at compliance with written rules: we must also measure the behaviour of our politicians against the attitudes and opinions of the public. But where does the public draw the boundary between acceptable and unacceptable conduct? More important, to avoid future problems, what types of behaviour are excusable, and what types will scandalize the public? There has been no shortage of polls about past ethical 'events' like the GST situation—the government even conducted its own in Sheila Copps's by-election. What we don't have is comprehensive information about the general ethical boundaries that Canadians have established and that politicians should be aware of in making ethical choices. In the next chapter we will begin trying to uncover this information.

"And don't waste your time canvasssing the whole building,
young man. We think alike."

Chapter Two

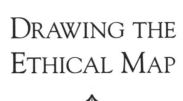

DRAWING THE ETHICAL MAP

The idea that rules, standards, and principles are the theoretical bases for sound ethical judgements is a perspective that can be traced to the early development of democracy in ancient Greece. But in classical Athens, the politicians were directly responsible to each and every citizen.[1] The political unit was small enough that everyone could vote on every issue and contribute to any debate. In modern democracies populations are so large that the governors are more remote from the governed and representation takes the place of direct participation. This introduces some practical complexities. What happens, for example, if elected representatives turn out to be ethically out of step with the people they represent? And how can we tell?

It is theoretically feasible, although quite impractical, to discuss questions of ethics at length and in depth with the one thousand or so members of Canada's various legislatures and come away with a good sense of their underlying principles and motives. With 30 million citizens this is out of the question. What we *can* do is survey the attitudes and opinions of a representative sample and use statistical methods to extend our findings to the country as a whole. This is essentially the method of survey research. One feature of this method is that it gives shape to citizens' opinions on ethical issues but does not delve into the process by which they came to those conclusions.

This type of attitudinal research is really the third and most recent wave of inquiry into corruption and political ethics. The first wave consisted of theoretical discussions of relevant principles; the second featured detailed dissection of particular cases, as the need for practical understanding of the complex issues became apparent. Case studies have clarified some particularly tricky scandals and provided some general insight, but they haven't really resolved much of the confusion about what is and is not acceptable. The advantage of survey methods is that they can probe general attitudes as well as specific instances. They also offer practical information that can be applied to the reform of political institutions. If the public is truly dissatisfied with its elected officials, it only makes sense to try to find out precisely what makes it unhappy, and thereby help the efforts to improve the situation. If our final destination is a more open and honourable political system, we need a good ethical map of the country.

STUDYING POLITICAL ETHICS AND CORRUPTION

In the last chapter we set down the large-scale features of this map—the democratic principles that underlie our system of government—and some sketchy internal boundaries—the rules and restrictions that attempt to regulate the behaviour of our officials. Before we can pull out our drafting tools and fill in the details, however, there are a few more conceptual hurdles to clear.

The Problem of Definition

Perhaps the main problem for studies of political ethics and corruption is definition. If you ask people whether they are in favour of corruption, virtually no one will say yes, but what exactly are they disapproving of? What does 'corrupt' mean? In the mouths of the media and politicians, it is used to mean everything from 'heinously evil' to 'happens to disagree with me'. Students of political ethics haven't been able to agree either, but three main categories of definitions have been proposed.

Legalistic definitions rely on the law and other formal rules to identify corruption. In this framework, 'corrupt' corresponds to 'illegal'. As noted, this can produce a very narrow definition of corruption; in fact, a system with few specific laws can appear to be almost free of corruption because what is not explicitly forbidden is not corrupt. This is not the sort of definition that most people would propose, since the way that the law applies is generally unclear to non-lawyers, and many citizens feel that what is right is not always the same as what is strictly legal. Interestingly enough, however, embattled public officials often seem to fall back on legalistic definitions when they try to explain away activities they are challenged on.

Another way of defining corruption is to conjure up the notion of the public interest. Corruption is behaviour that harms the public interest or betrays the public trust that politicians have a moral duty to uphold. In this wider type of definition mere compliance with the rules is not enough, and there are large areas of technically legal activity that none the less are harmful to the public interest. A problem with these definitions, however, is that they depend upon another slippery term: what exactly is the 'public interest', and how should it in turn be defined? Most conceptions are both broad and unclear, stretching from integrity in office to good management of public resources. If a government botches its economic policy, causing interest rates and unemployment to skyrocket, they have certainly harmed what most people think of as the public interest, but if the mistakes were honest misjudgements, were they really corrupt or just foolish? Will such a government be thrown out at the next election for some moral failing, or just for incompetence?

Definitions based on public opinion escape this problem of secondary definition by focusing on something more easily measured. People may not be able to supply a concrete definition of corruption that holds up under all circumstances, but just as with art and obscenity, they know it when they see it. In this scheme of things, the boundary between acceptable and unacceptable conduct is drawn by a simple yea-or-nay judgement.[2] In a sense, this definition encompasses the others, since some people may in fact be taking complex legal knowledge into account, while others may be referring to their own view of the public interest. Others may be basing their opinion on religious teachings, parental lessons, workplace standards, or just a 'gut feeling'. Some people just couldn't trust Brian Mulroney once they learned he owned so many pairs of Gucci loafers. Most people will probably combine all sorts of experience and inclination when they judge the acceptability of political behaviour.

The Importance of Attitudes and Opinions

The emphasis on public opinion and attitudes means that how the line between acceptable and unacceptable is drawn is less important than where it ends up, and how it varies between different subgroups. In a way, this is like an election: there are lots of competing theories about why people vote a certain way, but the total vote count is what matters in the end. Studying attitudes and opinions does not ignore the 'why'—there are subtle ways to compare overlapping opinions to reveal the reasoning behind them, but it concentrates on the more quantifiable and measurable 'where' and 'how much'.

In fact, we don't really know a great deal about what is acceptable and unacceptable to the Canadian public. Nor do politicians, who keep blundering into troublesome situations and scandals they apparently never foresaw. We have a good idea what really infuriates people (or at least what infuriates the media), and we know what people don't seem to worry too much about. What is missing is detailed information about the whole range in between. What activities can we expect Canadians to condemn and how much will they tolerate? How strong are these feelings and how widely shared? The answer may be different for different groups: is there a gender, generational, or geographic gap?

So how *do* we draw an ethical map of Canada? It will certainly be more complex than a simple roadmap, for there are numerous layers—the politician's view, the media's view, and so on—which sometimes seem to depict entirely different landscapes. Our goal is eventually to survey those as well, but we are starting with the fundamental geography, the terrain on which elections are fought, and the baseline on which all the others depend for support: the public. This map, with accurate contours of acceptability and unacceptability, can give the well-intentioned majority of politicians the guidance they need in order to avoid dangerous detours. It can also help to properly locate ethical guardrails—targeted rules and regulations that are needed to keep the less-well-intentioned few (or the confused) on course.

THE STUDY

We began to draw our map by assembling a team of political scientists with experience in both the technical aspects of survey methods and the philosophical intricacies of political ethics. We established a 'base camp' at the University of Guelph and developed a long-term strategy. Our first step was to assemble an inventory of the existing knowledge about and insight into ethical matters.

Asking the Experts

One source of expertise is the expanding body of academic research into political ethics. In the past few decades, attitudinal studies in this area, like ethical problems themselves, have proliferated, particularly in Canada, the United States, Britain, and

Australia which are often lumped together as the 'Anglo-American democracies'. Other studies have investigated systems in Europe, Japan, and the developing world.[3]

There have been two basic approaches, depending on what group is surveyed: 'elite' studies have focused on the opinions of small but powerful groups like politicians themselves, or journalists.[4] 'Mass' studies gauge the opinions of the general public.[5] Most work thus far has concentrated exclusively on one or the other level.[6] We decided to do both; that is, to pose the same questions to elites and to the public, and thus be able to compare their responses. This volume, however, will report only the information from the public survey.

Critics of this branch of research have emphasized what they believe are flaws in a definition of ethical acceptability based on public opinion. They consider such attitudes to be fleeting and unstable, prone to contradiction and fluctuation. Some have gone so far as to suggest that the fickleness revealed by opinion polls demonstrates that most of the public is confused about even basic political questions.[7] More recent work has disagreed with this conclusion, arguing that in some surveys measurement problems and simplistic assumptions have obscured the actually rather sophisticated public understanding of politics. This suggests that the public deserves more credit than it has got in the past.[8]

Certainly public opinion has its weaknesses as a basis for identifying ethical values, but as we have pointed out above, the alternatives are not perfect either. It is a common public impression that the law is not good at encapsulating ethical principles: loopholes in ethics rules big enough to drive a truck through contribute to public dissatisfaction and cynicism. And even if there are difficulties in measuring public opinion (which can be minimized by careful and rigorous survey design) it is hard to argue that survey results ought to be ignored in a democracy where the will of the people is what ultimately matters.

We were also determined to maintain a pragmatic emphasis for our work and to maximize the applicability of our results; that is, we wanted to create a map that people could actually use, not just hang on a wall and look at. To this end, we convened a gathering of individuals with direct experience in dealing with questions of political ethics. This ethics workshop[9] brought together politicians, businesspeople, journalists, lawyers, ethics practitioners, and leading researchers. There we presented our initial background studies and a draft questionnaire, and gathered many valuable suggestions. The comments of these practical experts highlighted areas of special concern and helped us perfect the wording and context of the questions we planned to ask.

Asking Canadians

The next step was to test our questionnaire in a pilot study.[10] Did it measure what we thought it would measure, and did we get the answers we expected? Yes and no. Our analysis of the results allowed us to refine and tighten our survey design and showed us which questions were hard to understand or easily misinterpreted. We also learned some valuable methodological lessons.[11]

The pilot study also revealed some interesting patterns in the way the responses clustered. As will be discussed later in the chapter, the many kinds of activity we asked about tended to organize themselves in the respondents' minds into four basic types. We tinkered with the survey to highlight these types, as well as to test the strength and significance of this categorization. For the most part, the pilot study demonstrated that we were on the right track—for one thing, people seemed especially eager to discuss their opinions of political ethics, as if they appreciated an outlet to vent their feelings.

Eventually, we were ready to administer our final survey to a large sample of voters across Canada. 'Interview central' was set up at the University of Guelph Development Office phone bank,

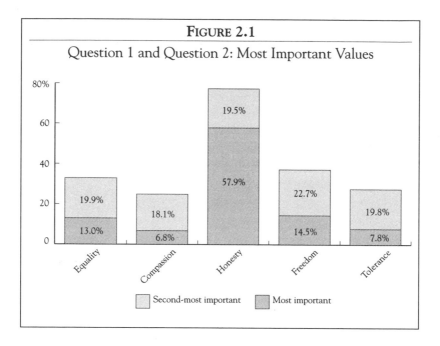

FIGURE 2.1

Question 1 and Question 2: Most Important Values

and a large pool of student interviewers, both anglophone and francophone, was assembled and trained.[12] Through the Institute for Social Research at York University, we obtained a randomized sample of phone numbers across Canada, stratified by region.[13] The sample thus provided a representative selection of households. In each household we contacted, the selection process was further randomized by having the interviewer ask to speak to the person 18 years of age or older who had had the most recent birthday.[14]

Each interview lasted about 35 minutes, but this was dependent upon how chatty the contacted individuals were. The student callers explained to the respondents that they were helping with a study of people's opinions about what politicians should or should not do, and promised to maintain confidentiality. We assured people that we were interested in their views. The response to our requests for assistance was wonderful. For

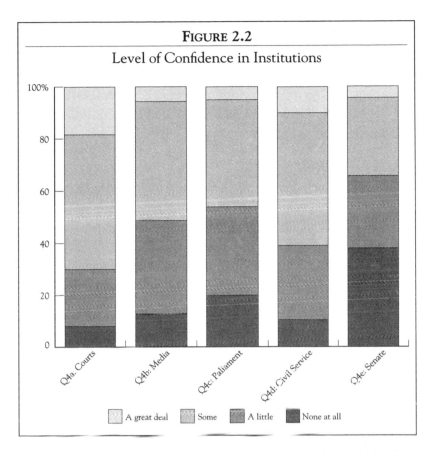

FIGURE 2.2

Level of Confidence in Institutions

the most part this proved to be a topic on which people had no trouble formulating and expressing opinions. The response rate was slightly over 45 per cent.[15] The schedule of interviews was completed within a six-week period in January and February 1996. The final sample size was 1,419 respondents.

The interviews began with some general questions that established an 'ethical baseline' (Q1 to 5 of the questionnaire, reproduced in full in the Appendix). We first asked the respondents about what values they considered important. Honesty was clearly the most favoured policy: 58 per cent of the sample chose it as the value most important to them, and almost another 20 per

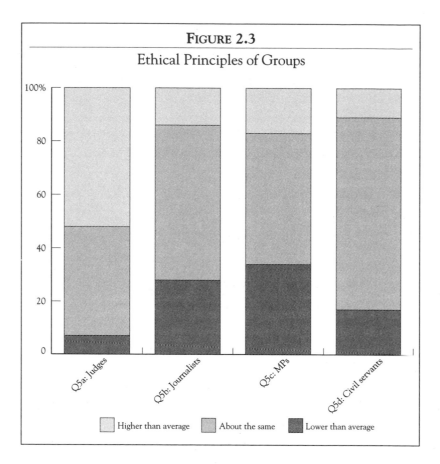

FIGURE 2.3

Ethical Principles of Groups

Q5a: Judges
Q5b: Journalists
Q5c: MPs
Q5d: Civil servants

☐ Higher than average   ▨ About the same   ■ Lower than average

cent chose it as second-most important (Figure 2.1). This is somewhat surprising, given that it was competing against other fundamental values like equality and freedom. Respondents were next
asked to indicate their level of confidence in various political
institutions and to assess the ethical principles of different types
of office holders. As recent studies of political institutions around
the globe have suggested, electorates have grown more and more
cynical about the performance of their leaders and the capacity
of their institutions to serve their interests.[16] Forty-one per cent
of the sample expressed only 'some' confidence in Parliament, 34

TABLE 2.1

Private Morality—'Things People Do'
'Usually', 'Sometimes', 'Rarely', or 'Never' acceptable

QUESTION

6a   Failing to report damage accidentally done to a parked car

6b   Paying cash to a plumber to avoid taxes

6c   Lying to protect a friend

6d   Accepting a gift for doing your job

6e   Not telling the whole truth to avoid embarrassment

6f   Claiming benefits which you are not entitled to

6g   Using your influence to get a friend a job

6h   Giving a police officer money to avoid a speeding ticket

6i   Not declaring to customs things brought in from another country

6j   Breaking a promise

per cent expressed 'a little', and a full 20 per cent said they had no confidence at all. The courts and the civil service fared better (Figure 2.2).

The next section of the questionnaire probed the respondents' own private moral attitudes (Table 2.1). Respondents were given a list of 'things that some people do' and were asked whether they thought each one was usually acceptable, sometimes acceptable, rarely acceptable, or never acceptable (Questions 6a to 6j). These items ranged from actual illegalities such as 'claiming benefits which you are not entitled to', to just socially 'tricky' acts like 'breaking a promise'. The reactions to these activities gave a good indication of a respondent's personal ethical code.

The next section of the questionnaire shifted the focus toward specific issues of political behaviour. We presented the

TABLE 2.2

Hypothetical Scenarios—Numeric Response (0–10)

	QUESTION	ABBREVIATION
7	A cabinet minister is seeing a psychiatrist and decides not to tell the Prime Minister about it.	*Psychiatrist*
8	An MP who has cancer denies this fact when asked by a journalist.	*Cancer*
9	The Prime Minister appoints a loyal party supporter to head the CBC.	CBC
11	A campaign worker is rewarded with a government job, for which he is fully qualified.	*Campaign worker*
12	At Christmas a Member of Parliament accepts a bottle of wine from a constituent who is grateful for help in speeding up the paperwork to get a passport.	*Wine*
14	On a trip to the Northwest Territories, a cabinet minister meets with a group of local artists who present him with a valuable carving. On his return, he displays the carving in his home.	*Carving*
15	An MP owns a local clothing store. He votes in favour of legislation to provide loans to small business.	*Store*
17	The Minister of Tourism owns a large hotel.	*Hotel*
18	The Minister of Agriculture owns a large farm.	*Farm*
19	A cabinet minister helps a builder get an important government contract. In return, the minister accepts the free use of the builder's cottage for a week.	*Contract*
21	A Senator who has no other outside employment, agrees to serve as a corporate director for a small fee.	*Director*

TABLE 2.2 CONTINUED	
Hypothetical Scenarios—Numeric Response (0–10)	
QUESTION	ABBREVIATION
22 An MP uses the parliamentary restaurant, where the prices are subsidized, to host dinners for visiting constituents.	Restaurant
24 After working late on constituency business, an MP takes a cab home and charges it to the government.	Cab ride
25 During an election campaign, a political party promises not to close any hospitals. After the election, the party finds it must close one hospital because of its deficit-reduction plan.	Hospital
27 A cabinet minister learns that his deputy minister is being secretly investigated by the RCMP. To protect the reputation of his deputy, the Minister claims to know nothing about the investigation when asked in Parliament.	RCMP

respondents with a series of vignettes or scenarios involving public officials (Table 2.2). It was made clear that these were hypothetical situations, although we did attempt to make them as realistic as possible. We asked people to indicate their opinion of the activities depicted, using a numerical scale from 0 to 10, where 0 meant totally unacceptable and 10 totally acceptable.[17] Some scenarios had a follow-up question that asked whether the respondent thought that people in politics do 'this sort of thing' frequently. Throughout, clarifications were strictly limited; although some respondents asked for more information, they were told they had to base their answer on what was provided. This helped to prevent the assumptions of the interviewers from influencing the survey results.

TABLE 2.3

Hypothetical Scenarios—Forced-Choice Response

QUESTION	ABBREVIATION
28 A cabinet minister is seeing a marriage counsellor. A journalist asks him if this is true. Should the minister say: (a) 'It's none of your business.' (b) 'Every marriage has its rough spots.' (c) 'Yes, I'm seeing a counsellor.'	*Marriage*
30 The Minister of Justice has to appoint a judge. Who should the minister consider: (a) Any qualified persons (b) Qualified persons who are loyal party members (c) Qualified persons selected by a non-partisan committee	*Judge*
34 The former Energy Minister is asked by his brother, who works for an oil company, for advice as to who to talk to about a tax break for his company. The former minister should: (a) be as helpful as possible (b) refer his brother to an industry consultant (c) say he's sorry, but he can't give any advice	*Brother*
36 A cabinet minister is faced with a large debt following his re-election. His advisers tell him that the best way to raise money is to invite people to a private breakfast meeting where anyone who pays $500 can talk to the minister about their concerns. Should the minister: (a) go along with the plan (b) set no fee, but encourage people to make donations (c) reject the idea	*Breakfast*

Table 2.3 continued

Hypothetical Scenarios—Forced-Choice Response

	QUESTION	ABBREVIATION
38	A minister *has* to attend an important meeting in Europe. He is issued a first-class plane ticket. His wife, who sees very little of her husband, would like to go along. Should the minister: (a) bring his wife along at his own expense (b) trade in his first class fare for two seats in economy (c) go alone	*Ticket*
40	The Minister of Finance is scheduled to make a major speech to international investors about the Canadian economy. At the last minute he learns that the deficit is much larger than expected. Should the minister: (a) present the new deficit estimates (b) cancel his speech (c) make the speech, and say nothing about the deficit	*Deficit*

After this group of 'acceptability rating' questions, we described some more scenarios, but this time we asked the respondents to tell us what they thought the official involved should do (Table 2.3). Specifically, they were given a choice of three possible responses. This type of question actually forces the respondent to enter into the situation described and to try to resolve it. Again, the follow-up question was whether the respondents thought that people in politics would make the same choice as they just had. Rating scales, like those in the first group of scenarios, have long been used in attitudinal studies of political corruption,[18] but this study represents the debut of 'forced-choice' questions. Both types of scenario questions seemed to be the most enjoyable parts of the interview.

TABLE 2.4

Attitudinal Statements
'Strongly disagree', 'Somewhat disagree',
'Somewhat agree', or 'Strongly agree'

QUESTION

42   No matter what we do, we can never put an end to political corruption in this country.

43   Politicians cannot expect to have the same degree of privacy as everyone else.

44   Political corruption is a widespread problem in this country.

45   Obedience and respect for authority are the most important virtues children should learn.

46   People who run for election are usually out for themselves.

47   The media say too much about the private lives of politicians.

48   We should not expect MPs to have higher ethical standards than the average person.

49   Journalists judge politicians by standards that journalists themselves don't meet.

50   What cabinet ministers do in their private lives tells us whether they would be good leaders.

51   People distrust politicians because they don't understand what politics is all about.

52   In general, politicians are very well-paid.

53   It is important to protect fully the rights of radicals.

54   Loyalty to friends is often more important than obeying the law.

55   No MP should be allowed to hold office for more than 10 years.

The formal survey was rounded out by a set of general attitudinal questions about politics and corruption (Table 2.4). Statements of opinion such as 'People who run for election are usually out for themselves' were presented, and the respondents were asked whether they strongly agreed, somewhat agreed, somewhat disagreed, or strongly disagreed. The questions probed their opinions about the degree of corruption in the country, the role of the media and their interest in the private lives of politicians, the standards of our officials, and their income. We also asked about some possibilities for change and proposed a number of reforms, asking whether they would reduce corruption a lot, a little, or not at all (Questions 58 to 63).

The final section of the questionnaire was dedicated to a standard series of socio-demographic questions, about age, income, education, religion, and so on; and questions intended to gauge the respondent's political awareness and knowledge (Questions 64 to 82). We also asked if the respondent supported a particular party in general, as well as the usual short-term-preference question 'If an election were held today, whom would you vote for?' We didn't have to ask where the respondents lived (the area code of the phone number told us that), and barring a few embarrassing cases caused by ambiguous names or tones of voice, it was clear whether the respondent was male or female.

Interpreting the Answers

One way of making sense of 1400 different opinions is to recognize informal impressions. We all do this in daily life, as we discuss various issues with various people and get an idea of what other people think and how it compares with our own views. Our interviewers certainly got a good sense (in some cases, quite an earful) of what many Canadians think about political ethics, especially some examples of particularly offensive behaviour we described to them. But in order to go beyond this kind of intuitive, subjective description and produce systematic, justifiable conclusions about public attitudes, we need to resort to statistics and empirical analysis.

The word 'statistics' can be a formidable barrier to many readers. Those who are interested in the details of our analysis can read all the endnotes and will be interested in our forthcoming, more formal analysis of this study and its companions.[19] However, statistics are really just the use of mathematics to detect and describe patterns. Given a pile of 'raw' data, statistical techniques allow us to pick out tendencies and relationships that might be invisible to the naked eye. At the same time, they allow us to see through and reject apparent patterns that are really just misleading coincidences. Statistical tools allow us not just to identify the 'average' response, but also to measure how 'concentrated' the responses are, that is, whether most people generally agree, or whether the answers are all over the map. There are also statistical techniques to uncover how and to what degree certain questions are linked, that is, the extent to which they tend to be answered in the same way (all yes or all no, for example) by different people.[20]

One technical notion that we will not be able to avoid is the idea that a result is 'statistically significant'. This means essentially that a statistical test has shown mathematically that the pattern described is almost certainly 'real' and not just the result of chance. In the fine print of opinion polls, there is always some disclaimer to the effect that the results are accurate to within plus or minus so many percentage points, 19 times out of 20. This is a statement of how statistically significant the results are. The same customary cut-off point of 95 per cent certainty will be used throughout our analysis unless otherwise specified. In other words, as in any other study of human preferences, we cannot be absolutely sure that the patterns we identify are real, but we can be sure that we are right at least 95 times out of 100.[21] In many cases we will be able to do even better.

For the most part we will avoid the details of the statistical tests that underlie our conclusions and concentrate on the outlines of the results. We will state the percentage of respondents who agreed or disagreed, and so on. When dealing with the scenario items, we will describe all scores from 0 to 4 as generally indicating an 'unacceptable' attitude, and 6 to 10 as a generally 'acceptable' response. Five would of course be completely neutral. For some analyses, it is more revealing to refer to the 'mean score' of the respondents. This is simply the formal name for 'average'.[22] If the difference between mean scores for two items is statistically significant, we can confidently conclude that the one is seen as distinctly more (or less) acceptable than the other.

One type of pattern our analysis brought out was the identification of divergent sub-groups. No one needs to be reminded that 'the average Canadian' is only a convenient fiction. There are fault lines criss-crossing our society in every which way, and on either side people can have quite divergent opinions. Between men and women for example lies a 'gender gap'. From academic studies to pop-psych Mars-Venus formulations, it has been argued that men and women see many things differently.[23] Does this apply to political ethics as well? Other important divides are regional and generational. The long and tumultuous history of unquiet Confederation means that Canadians tend to assume automatically that people in different regions react in wildly different ways. And should we expect twenty-somethings to have the same views as their parents and grandparents?

The characteristics that divide the sample into sub-groups are referred to as 'independent variables', because they are characteristics of the survey respondents that are independent of what questions we ask or how we ask them. Previous attitudinal studies have highlighted several independent variables as 'correlates of corruption attitudes': important indicators of opinion that display a prevailing directional trend.[24] In some studies, for example, women have been stricter than men in their judgements of political behaviour and less tolerant of questionable activity. Many arguments have been advanced to explain this tendency: women have historically been excluded from politics and thus may be less willing to overlook the little bits of dirt that so often get swept under the rug. Or perhaps the competitive, antagonistic, self-oriented nature of politics, which lurks beneath most ethical issues, is essentially male and thus alien to women.[25] It is important to note that surveys have told us only that women are on average more critical; the explanations are only theories that may explain this tendency.

Age is a variable that has produced conflicting results. Early studies suggested that the young were more critical than the old; more recent work has claimed the opposite. An interesting possibility is that the apparent contradiction is actually due just to the maturing of the population: those who were young in the early studies are now 20 years older. As the baby boom ages, the demographic centre of gravity of our population shifts.

In Canada, regional variation has been used to explain almost everything, and ethical attitudes are no different. A traditional view associates the Maritimes and Quebec with problems like questionable electoral practices (vote-buying), reliance on patronage, and over-powerful political machines like those of Duplessis and Smallwood. In this view, these regions would be expected to display a more favourable attitude toward such behaviour. In the other direction, there is some empirical basis for the stereotype of austere prairie populism. According to one study, western MPs were less tolerant of conflict of interest and constituency service than their colleagues from other parts of the country.[26] We will see whether the overall ethical 'tilt' of the country follows this pattern.

In our study, we explored the influence of these and other possible independent variables. Some, such as socio-economic status, religion, education, and ideology, did not play a consistent or significant role. The three variables we concentrated on were:

gender, region, and age. Dividing respondents into gender categories needs no explanation. For analysing geographic variation, we used five regions: British Columbia, the West, Ontario, Quebec, and the Atlantic provinces.

Categorization by age is a bit more complicated. We wanted more detail than simply old versus young, but a large number of narrow age groups quickly becomes unwieldy. We needed a small number of categories that could be easily labelled and recognized. This meant age groups of roughly generational scope (20 to 30 years), and we have thus classified people as Elders (born in 1945 or earlier), Baby Boomers (born 1946–65), or Generation Xers (born since 1966). These same labels have been used elsewhere to characterize the generations as distinct subcultures with different sets of values.[27] We use them primarily as a convenient and obvious organizational tool. It is in general difficult to establish that a 'generation gap' is strictly a product of demographic shifts (the young are the way they are because of the times they grew up in) rather than life-cycle effects (the young are that way simply because they are young, and as they age they will change as their elders did). In most cases, both forms of explanation are entirely plausible.

Before we could use these three variables, we also had to establish that they were also 'orthogonal', that is, that they vary independently of one another and do not in some way reflect the same pattern. For example, if by chance we had interviewed only older women and younger men, then gender and age would not be orthogonal, and it would not be valid to ascribe some variation to a sex difference, since the same differential might really be caused by an age effect. We found in fact some correlation between age and region (gender was completely independent). In part this reflects the fact that the generations are not distributed evenly across the country: many Ontarians retire to British Columbia, and many young people have left the Atlantic provinces because of the economic difficulties of that region. In any case, whenever we examined either regional or generational effects, we performed additional tests that controlled for the effects of one on the other to establish that the trends we identify in the following chapters are valid for each variable independently.

Types of Ethical Dilemmas

The other major kind of pattern we can discern in the results has to do with the type of behaviour depicted. We confronted our respondents with a range of specific activities, but people don't react to every situation on a completely *ad hoc* basis, as if it were unrelated to any other. Similar situations tend to elicit similar responses, and there are patterns of responses that suggest that people employ underlying mental rules and conceptual classifications to help them make judgements. Thus, for example, cheating on your taxes is fundamentally related to, but more serious than, pocketing some cash dropped by a stranger.

Some patterns, like this one, are easy to detect just by thinking about them. More subtle patterns can be revealed by statistical tools such as factor analysis.[28] These tools can also provide a numerical justification for more obvious and expected patterns. Our analysis of the pilot study suggested four important factors or types of ethically dubious behaviour. Each of the four—conflict of interest, gifts and gains, patronage, and lying—have important places as sub-categories in the study of corruption and ethics; books have been written about each one. This classification suggests that people tend to evaluate various instances of lying in a consistent manner and that therefore it is possible to say someone is in general 'critical' or 'forgiving' of lies. But this doesn't necessarily provide any insight into how that person might view conflict of interest or patronage. Our revision of the questionnaire for the final survey was in part designed to flesh out this four-fold categorization.

The final pattern we investigated was the gradation of answers within each type. Do large gifts elicit a more critical response than smaller ones? When a politician does a special favour for someone, does it matter whether the recipient is a constituent? This notion of 'dimensions' of unacceptability—important characteristics of an act that influence how it is viewed—has played a central role in attitudinal studies of ethics.[29] It also reflects the murkiness of politics in the real world, where officials face ethical dilemmas routinely. These arise both from the nature of their responsibilities and from the opportunities linked to their position. Politics is a game of hard choices and often there is no one clear course of action. It is the particular aspects of a situation—the mitigating variables—that help to distinguish the lesser of two evils. Our questionnaire employs these dimensions and varies them throughout. We invite the reader to watch for how differences in the specific details of activities affect the way they are evaluated.

The next four chapters will describe these patterns and the ways in which they express themselves in detail. We will look at each type of behaviour separately, examining degrees of tolerance and mitigation: the shades of grey between different kinds of lies or different techniques of patronage. We will also examine who is especially tolerant or especially critical of each kind of behaviour, and what the reasons may be. Ultimately we will approach the broader questions of how much agreement there really is among Canadians about what constitutes 'the right thing to do', and how critical we are of our politicians' decisions. Some answers will come as no surprise; others may show that the conventional wisdom is not always so wise.

John Larter cartoon from *The Toronto Star*, 2 September 1988.
Reprinted with permission - The Toronto Star Syndicate.

Chapter Three

✧

CONFLICT
OF INTEREST

✦

We have all seen the headlines: 'Minister Accused of Conflict of Interest,' 'Conflict of Interest Case Haunts Government.' Headline writers like to treat conflict of interest as if it were a crime, blaring out their suspicions and accusations but paying much less attention to how the conflict arose in the first place or what actually constitutes a conflict of interest. Yet those are the most important issues in any conflict-of-interest case.

The fact is that most of us will experience serious conflicts of interest in our lives. Conflicts arise when there is a clash between two roles we are playing, such as friend and banker, or teacher and entrepreneur. If you are going to court in a child-custody dispute, you don't ask your mother to be your lawyer, even if she is a child-custody expert. And, if you're smart, you don't follow the advice of investment consultants who have just returned from a trip to Hawaii paid for by a large mutual fund company. Your mother and your investment counsellor are in conflict-of-interest situations. The behaviour expected of one's mother is not consistent with that expected of one's lawyer. What people need from their lawyer is sound, dispassionate advice. No matter how professional your mother is, she is in no position to supply that to you. And no matter how professional your investment counsellor is, once he accepts a trip to Hawaii as a gratuity, his advice on mutual fund investment is compromised by his obligation to repay his generous friends in the mutual fund industry.

These are conflicts of interest that we can avoid by not asking people to compromise themselves and by not dealing with people who are compromised. Some conflicts, however, can't be avoided. The school board trustee whose daughter gets a job as a teacher did not create this situation. But neither can he be totally dispassionate about teachers' salaries. The police officer who pulls over his best friend's son can't credibly claim that this friendship will have no effect on what happens next. Somehow these people must remove themselves from the situation at the earliest possible moment, or find a way to separate the duties of one role (as father or friend), from those of the other (trustee or police officer).

For politicians (and other public office holders such as the trustee and the police officer above), the stakes in a role conflict are higher for two reasons. First, political offices are public property, and the way the holders of those offices perform their duties have effects well beyond the private domains in which most of us live. Politicians who fail to separate their private interests from their public duties, or who fail to place their duties above their personal interest, bring discredit not just to themselves, but also to their office.

And while the same might be said of the lawyer who advises his client to invest in mortgages he holds, or the doctor who refers patients to a clinic she owns, the consequences are much broader when public offices are involved. In such cases, it is not only politicians as a whole whose reputations are damaged, but the institutions of politics and the political community as a whole. Democratic practice rests heavily on the electorate's faith in the fundamental integrity of its political leaders. As Watergate demonstrated, when that faith begins to unravel, there is no 'stop rule' that prevents the degradation from infecting the entire political system.

The second reason that conflicts of interest are so problematic for politicians is that the public offices they occupy and the functions they perform all rest on the rule of law. The rule of law states that every citizen is equal before the law and deserves unbiased treatment.[1] There are no special deals. Conflicts of interest create situations in which politicians are tempted to become beholden to private interests, making it impossible for them to perform their public responsibilities in an unbiased fashion.[2]

The private interest they are beholden to may be their own—when, for example, a politician arranges a government contract for his company—but that is not always the case. A politician can become beholden to someone else by accepting a gift or a position or campaign support. The gift giver may never ask the politician for anything in return, in which event no actual conflict occurs, but the moment the giver does ask or the politician thinks he is asking, then the politician's judgement is affected. It is no longer possible to treat the request the same way as anyone else's. This is a conflict of interest.

Of course politicians, like the rest of us, have private interests and personal friends. And while most politicians are aware that making public decisions that directly affect their own private interest is a conflict, these same politicians will be tempted to accept gifts or positions or support or information from their friends. Of course, having friends is crucial to achieving political success, but when politicians use their public office to influence the political process in their own private interest or in the interests of the friends to whom they feel indebted, the rule of law is compromised and a conflict of interest is established.

EXCUSES FOR CONFLICTS OF INTEREST

None of this is clear-cut. It is not always clear, for example, just when politicians are acting in their official role and when they are acting in a private capacity. Similarly, it is not always clear that a politician's judgement has been clouded or that anyone has benefited privately from a public decision. Ambiguity abounds, and it is in this ambiguity that politicians take refuge. Let's consider some of the more popular excuses for conflict of interest.

Ignorance

As silly as it may seem, there are many politicians who believe that if they simply say they were unaware of the rules or that they were unclear on the concept they will be forgiven or at least given a second chance. Take the case of Bill Vander Zalm and Fantasy Gardens. As Premier of British Columbia, Vander Zalm clearly had highly visible, time-consuming, public duties to perform. Being premier is not an obscure, part-time job. The size of the job and its public prominence mean that there is almost no room for the Premier to play other roles, except perhaps as scout leader or church usher. Beyond these narrowly confined tasks, the Premier can perform very few public roles as an ordinary citizen and not as the Premier of British Columbia.

It seems that Vander Zalm didn't know that. When he embarked on the sale of Fantasy Gardens, his private family enterprise, he invited international investors to visit the premises and while there be entertained at the expense of the B.C. taxpayer. He made interventions with other business people and accepted a cash payment of $20,000, ostensibly for his assistance in obtaining the sale of an adjacent property.[3] In other words, Vander Zalm completely mixed his private and public responsibilities. And when confronted with the clear evidence of this, he defended himself by maintaining that his actions in connection with Fantasy Gardens were entirely unaffected by his actions as Premier of the province. The Conflict of Interest Commissioner, Ted Hughes, didn't agree. But he did at least credit Vander Zalm (if credit is the right word) with an 'apparently sincere belief that no conflict existed so long as the public wasn't aware of what was going on.'[4]

It is painful to watch someone, either implicitly or explicitly, use ignorance as an excuse. Yet in some situations, it may be true that the official involved genuinely does not perceive any conflict. As we will see below, however, Canadians are unimpressed with such politicians.

The Conflict Is Only 'Potential'

We said above that conflicts of interest are part of life and that any one of us may find ourselves in one without even trying. So, it is possible for politicians to argue that there is no 'real' conflict, only a 'potential' one, and that potential conflicts should not be matters of criticism or condemnation.

This is a good argument, up to a point. As mentioned in Chapter 1, the federal government's code of conduct for politicians and senior public servants does not outlaw potential conflicts. If it did, no one would be able to go into politics. But the code does say that holders of public office should 'perform their official duties and arrange their private affairs in such a manner that public confidence and trust in the integrity, objectivity and impartiality of government are conserved and enhanced' (sec. 7(a)). Notice the word 'enhanced'. It's not enough just to obey the law. Problems must be anticipated before they occur. Politicians must have foresight; otherwise they will have to struggle to extricate themselves from some situation they thought would never happen. This spectacle hardly ever 'enhances' public confidence and trust in government.

Mr Justice Parker, in his examination of the troubles of Sinclair Stevens, described potential conflict as 'that momentary oasis of sober reflection that allows the public office holder an opportunity to respond to and resolve the problem.'[5] It is in this oasis that the politician is expected to recognize that a potential conflict of interest is on the verge of becoming something real. Unfortunately, too many politicians don't take the time to think the issues through. They feel overwhelmed by all the files they have to read, the meetings they have to attend, and the policy decisions they have to reach. They plough ahead because, as politicians, they are used to acting decisively. When politicians have decisions to make, they're not in the mood for reflecting on their other roles or their personal interests. The time for reflection is on the eve of the election. Embarking on a political career means sizing up your vulnerabilities. In 1984, shortly after being appointed Minister of Industrial and Regional Expansion in the cabinet of Brian Mulroney, Stevens placed some of his assets in a blind trust. Presumably he did so to avoid the possibility that later on, in the course of his public duties, he would find himself acting in a manner that affected his private interests. As minister of a department in charge of industry, Stevens was more likely than most to become entangled in public decisions that would affect his family business, the York Centre group of companies, in which he had strong ownership and transactional interests.

The blind trust is a form of divestment. Although Stevens didn't actually sell his assets, the idea behind a blind trust is that the owner has no knowledge of what happens to his assets. They can be sold and other assets bought, for example, without his knowledge. That's the theory. In Stevens's case, Justice Parker determined that Stevens 'knew about and was involved with the York Centre companies and thus with the trust assets, because his wife and his special assistant told him about the trust assets, and because his wife participated in joint management of the assets with him.'[6] So much for divestment and the momentary pause for sober reflection.

In our research on attitudes toward conflict of interest, we didn't ask about blind trusts, but we did ask about potential conflicts. Ministers of Agriculture who own farms and Ministers of Tourism who own hotels are in potential conflict. Is this a serious problem? Is the fact that these are merely potential conflicts an adequate excuse for neglecting to deal with them?

The Conflict Is Only 'Apparent'

Politicians occasionally argue that some conflicts of interest are apparent, not real, and if no real conflict exists there is no need to correct or deal with it. Most codes of conduct for politicians are unsympathetic to this point of view. Since the publication in 1973 of the Green Paper entitled *Members of Parliament and Conflict of Interest*, most codes have instructed politicians to avoid appearances of conflict of interest just as much as the real thing. The Green Paper defined conflict of interest as a 'situation in which a Member of Parliament has a personal or private pecuniary interest sufficient to influence, *or appear to influence*, the exercise of his public duties and responsibilities.'[7] But neither the Green Paper nor subsequent codes paused to explain what actually constitutes the appearance of conflict. It was not until the Parker Commission that appearance was defined as a 'reasonable apprehension'. Appearance of conflict exists when there is a reasonable apprehension, by reasonably informed persons, that a conflict of interest exists.[8]

Of course, what is reasonable for one person may not be reasonable for another. When Premier Ralph Klein of Alberta opened the Hong Kong office of an Alberta company, Multi-Corp, he undoubtedly thought he was promoting Albertan entrepreneurs. When his wife, Colleen, subsequently accepted 10,000 Multi-Corp shares at below market value without having to pay for them, he probably thought it was sufficient to declare the existence of the shares. And when these shares sky-rocketed in value on the Alberta Stock Exchange, he assumed that he and his wife had legitimately earned a nest egg that would help them in their retirement.

The opposition parties thought otherwise and demanded an investigation by the Ethics Commissioner. Klein, who was apoplectic at the accusations, declared that he would resign if the investigation turned up even a hint of wrongdoing. As he explained it, what he did for Multi-Corp he would do for any other Alberta company interested in marketing its products abroad. But would anyone else, other than Multi-Corp executives, have been able to obtain the deal that Mrs Klein obtained? That was the problem, that and the fact that Mr Klein failed to tell the Ethics Commissioner about the terms on which the shares had been received.

Would a reasonably informed person have a reasonable apprehension of a conflict? Anyone looking in on this situation would have to wonder if the people who arranged for Mrs Klein to benefit handsomely (for an investment she didn't really make) may not have acquired a 'reasonable' expectation of favourable treatment the next time they wanted something from the Government of Alberta. And even if they had no such expectation, the 'reasonable' Albertan may be forgiven for concluding that they had.

In the next section we report on survey questions concerning politicians who appear to have had their independence compromised by accepting personal favours or income. In these cases we do not stipulate a quid pro quo, but merely indicate that someone appears to be beholden to someone else. The results suggest that the authors and promoters of codes of conduct are right when they argue that the appearance of conflict is as damaging as the real thing and that politicians must take reasonable steps to avoid it.

The Public and Private Interests Coincide

A politician is elected from a local constituency and goes to the capital to look out for the constituency's interest. Public works like harbours, causeways, and trade centres are traditional slabs of 'bacon' for politicians to bring home when seeking to earn the recognition and gratitude of their constituents. Constituents also welcome the creative placement of contracts for public services and grants to businesses that locate in the area. Politicians who want to be re-elected try hard to obtain these goodies or at least to be available for interviews when they are announced.

Although the spectacle of politicians lining up to take credit for spending the taxpayers' money is somewhat unseemly, surely it can't be considered a conflict of interest. Not usually. Sometimes, however, politicians find themselves supporting something that their constituents want but that will also provide personal benefits to the politician. Everyone benefits. If interests coincide, can they also conflict?

In their 1984 report on conflict of interest, Mitchell Sharp and Michael Starr observed, 'the public interest could be abused equally where the private interests of the office holder coincide with the public interests so as to mesh together, with the result that in serving the public purpose the individual benefits privately as well.'[9] So, conflict of interest doesn't necessarily require conflicting interests. Where the public interest is served and benefits are widely diffused, politicians who benefit at the same time may be in conflict.

When she was Minister of Housing in the government of Ontario Premier Bob Rae, Evelyn Gigantes became embroiled in a public-housing controversy in her own constituency. Members of a non-profit housing enterprise had fallen out with one another and were threatening law suits and political action. Gigantes was trying to avert a conspicuous legal battle. If she had succeeded in getting all the parties to the dispute to drop their charges, it is likely that everyone, including Gigantes, would have benefited. In this case, of course, her benefit would have been political rather than personal.

Unfortunately, Evelyn Gigantes encountered two problems. First, Bob Rae's code of conduct explicitly forbade ministers from getting involved in local matters that were before the courts. No court proceedings had begun, but Gigantes's plea for all sides to 'back off all actions against the other'[10] was interpreted by some as intimidation. Second, her involvement was judged, by a lawyer hired to study the matter, as likely to undermine public confidence and trust in the administration of justice.

Gigantes resigned, to save the government further embarrassment she said, but she insisted she had done nothing wrong. There is no doubt that she would have benefited politically if she could have settled the public housing dispute out of court. But then, most of the parties to the conflict would have benefited as well. The problem is that ministers of the Crown are more than constituency healers; they have other roles to play. The roles of political fixer and of cabinet minister are not always compatible, and occasionally one of them has to take second place. Those looking in on these conflicts usually think that the role of impartial administrator should override that of constituency servant.[11]

Ordinary politicians, that is those who are not ministers and so don't have to worry about applying rules and administering programs may not feel the conflict between roles quite so directly. There are still situations, however, in which they stand to benefit, along with many others, from a decision they participate in. If the decision is the passage of a piece of legislation, as in the case outlined below, they are making this decision in company with many others. Does any of this matter? Are Canadians inclined to say that this kind of thing is inevitable, or should politicians find ways to avoid even these kinds of conflicts, where they have had little say in putting the legislation together and their benefit is shared with thousands of others?

CANADIANS EVALUATE CONFLICTS OF INTEREST

Politicians are expected to be ambitious. Most of them don't run for office in order to lose. And when they are elected, they often hope to be ministers one day, or at least to be re-elected. In a sense, then, politicians do look out for themselves. This is not necessarily bad; in fact ambitious politicians are often the ones who pay closest attention to what their constituents want. Even people who are out for themselves can do a good job, and some would go as far as to argue that those who aren't looking out for number one can't look after anybody else either.

Of course, it is one thing for politicians to look out for themselves and another thing to do so in an unethical manner. The conflict-of-interest issues we have discussed bring politicians very close to the edge. They may not always be acting in their own interest, but at the very least some of them seem prepared to tolerate conflicts and then look for excuses. But as we have already pointed out, this willingness to take chances, ignore 'apparent' conflicts, or allow 'potential' conflicts to fester is far more damaging and dangerous for politicians than for ordinary citizens. The stakes are higher because the whole political system is affected when judgements are poor.

Canadians agree with this perspective. Should MPs be expected to have the same standards as the average person (Q48)? Over half of the respondents to our survey (57 per cent) thought that the same standards were not enough (Figure 3.1). That still leaves a large proportion of Canadians who are content with the standards of the 'average person'. Assuming these standards are high and ethical lapses are few and far between, there will be no problems. But as we probe deeper into public attitudes, it is evident that Canadians will not tolerate openly compromised positions.

'Actual' Conflicts

Remember that conflicts arise when elected officials juggle their roles. A cabinet minister who is responsible for handing out contracts is acting as a government decision maker. The same minister, in planning a vacation, must not be tempted to accept

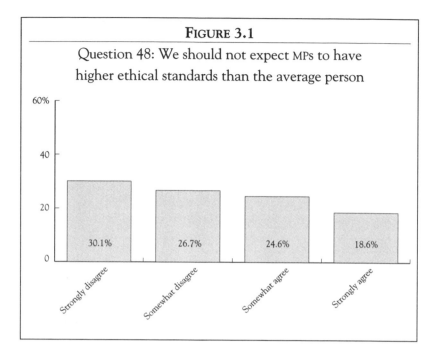

FIGURE 3.1

Question 48: We should not expect MPs to have higher ethical standards than the average person

offers of condos or holidays from the people whose economic fates he or she is helping to decide. Keep the roles of decision maker and vacationer completely separate, and conflicts can be avoided. Failure to do so creates the impression that politicians are receiving pay-offs for doing their job, something that falls clearly within the classic definition of conflict of interest.

Canadians have no trouble at all in recognizing and condemning this kind of conflict of interest. In Q19, a cabinet minister helps a builder get an important government contract, and in return the minister accepts the free use of the builder's cottage for a week. An overwhelming 53 per cent of respondents found this behaviour to be totally unacceptable (0 on the 0 to 10 scale; Figure 3.2). Here the quid pro quo is so blatant and substantial that fewer than 10 per cent of respondents found the action acceptable to any degree.

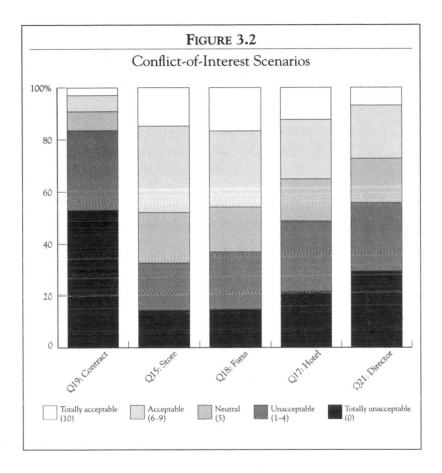

FIGURE 3.2

Conflict-of-Interest Scenarios

In the case of the local clothing-store owner who is also an MP, there is still an obvious conflict. You can't be a store owner and an MP and expect that these two roles will always be separate from one another. In Q15 we ask how people feel about this MP voting in favour of legislation to provide loans to small businesses. Notice that in this case the pay-off is implicit, not explicit. But the clear implication is that the MP who votes for the legislation stands to benefit. There are two real differences. First, the MP is not the only beneficiary. The store-owning MP is only one of thousands of store owners, and to a large extent the MP's private interests as a store owner are widely shared. The kind of special treatment enjoyed by the vacationing minister is not to be found in this situation. Put another way, Premier Vander Zalm's situation was not the same as Evelyn Gigantes's. Second, the personal benefit is not assured, because presumably not every store in the country will get a loan, and the MP's store may not even apply for one, much less receive it.

The responses to this question show that this situation is more ambiguous for respondents. Whereas virtually all respondents condemned the cottage pay-off, only 14 per cent found the store-owning MP's behaviour 'totally unacceptable' (a score of 10 on the 10-point scale). Interestingly enough, the same percentage found the behaviour totally acceptable, and quite a few found it moderately acceptable. Two other factors might help explain the response. In this scenario there is no identifiable donor of the benefit (technically one might say the government is the donor, but the point is that no external party appears to be influencing the MP's decision). Moreover, there is a sense of inevitability: one can hardly expect the member to vote against the legislation simply because he owns a store that might benefit. While one might expect the MP to abstain, he might respond that he is simply doing his job, that is, voting on behalf of and in the interest of store owners in his constituency, or even storekeepers throughout Canada.

The respondents had little difficulty identifying conflicts that involve direct pay-offs for specific benefits. But when the benefit is indirect and diffuse, there is no readily identifiable donor, and the MP's private interests are in accord with the public good, the responses are much more diverse. To remove himself from the conflict the MP would have to sell his store, which may well have been in his family for generations. This seems a heavy price to pay, all because a private interest happens to coincide with the interest of a public group.

'Potential' and 'Apparent' Conflicts

Potential conflicts of interest are a product of a situation that has not been created by the politician but that arises in the course of performing public duties. The clearest example is the politician who owns a farm and is appointed Minister of Agriculture. Like Sinclair Stevens, this MP might assume that his background in farming will help him to discharge his duties as minister. And it probably will. No one said Sinclair Stevens was a lousy Minister of Industry because he didn't know anything about industry.

Eventually however, this minister, like Stevens, may discover that being a farmer can be a disadvantage or even a liability. Unless he decides to sell his farm or put it in a (now discredited) blind trust, he is going to benefit, like a lot of other people, from the action of the ministry, assuming the Department of Agriculture is still working on behalf of farmers.

The respondents seem to understand this, but remarkably enough, many of them are not too worried about the problem. Perhaps they see the problem as too far in the future, or too theoretical, to get upset about. When asked whether they find it acceptable or unacceptable for the Minister of Agriculture to own a farm, about 40 per cent come down on the acceptable side (Figure 3.2). These respondents may still have their doubts about the situation (only 17 per cent say that it is 'totally acceptable') but there is a range of tolerance here that belies the problems commonly attributed to potential conflicts. Perhaps these respondents think that there are not many situations in which ministers will benefit directly; perhaps they aren't worried about the appearance of the situation since it has been something of a tradition in Canadian politics to appoint farmers as agriculture ministers; or maybe they are sentimental about the symbolism of the family farm and the wholesome images it conjures up.

Indeed, when we changed the Ministry and the holding to something less sentimental and more lucrative, there was a distinct shift toward unacceptability. Almost half the respondents felt it was improper for the Minister of Tourism to own a large hotel (scores of 0 to 4 on the scale). Hospitality services, like agriculture, are important industries in Canada, but farmers are working hard to put food on the nation's tables, whereas hoteliers may be seen as catering to less essential leisure activities. In fact, small family-owned hotels and huge industrialized agri-business operations belie both of these images. None the less, in the minds of some a distinction remains: running a hotel is a business; farming is a way of life. Even though the two hypothetical ministers are in essentially identical situations of potential conflict, the farmer seems to have a larger reservoir of public support to draw upon.

People are much more decisive when the situation is pushed even further toward exclusivity and profit. Question 21 features a Senator who serves as a paid member of a company's board of directors. Directorships, like Senate seats, are positions open only to a select few, and exactly how that selection is made and precisely what qualifies a person for these posts is often murky and subjective. Both are also tainted by the suspicion that they offer big money for little actual work. Only 21 per cent found this situation acceptable in any measure, and almost 30 per cent found it 'totally unacceptable'.

There the same potential for conflict exists as in the other two situations (we have no reason to assume that the directorship will automatically compromise the Senator's judgement, but it may) with the additional undercurrent of a possibly unearned benefit. Even if the public interest is never harmed, would the Senator have been appointed to the board if he or she had not been a public official?[12] It is important to realize that appearances are crucial here. The Senator's directorship fee may be quite appropriate to the value of the advice and services he or she renders to the company, and those services may have nothing whatsoever to do with the Senator's public responsibilities. On the other hand, the company may have expectations of favouritism just as explicit as the builder with the cottage. It is always difficult to sort out precarious but legitimate situations from simply well-disguised illegitimate schemes. This problem affects apparent conflicts of interest as well, but from a different angle. An apparent conflict of interest is a situation that may not in fact be a conflict but for one reason or another resembles one. Note that in the case of the potential conflict of interest, the official is in a position to exploit his or her office but can choose not to. In the case of apparent conflict there may not even be a conflict to begin with, but the appearance of the situation suggests the possibility of unsavoury conduct. A legitimate transaction can sometimes look like a questionable scheme. The paradox of apparent conflicts is that what actually happens becomes much less important than what the public—or at least certain 'attentive publics' like the media—thinks has happened.

Let's look at an example. In Q32 an MP helps a local restaurant owner get a liquor licence. A few weeks later, the owner sends the MP a cheque for $5,000. This is a very tricky scenario: there is nothing to suggest that the MP's help was anything other than the standard sort of constituency work that members do regularly, indeed are expected to do for people in their ridings. The arrival of the cheque, however, converts this innocuous act into what might appear to be a serious breach: a kickback, or influence peddling by an MP. Had the payment been a condition of the MP's involvement, this situation would be equivalent to Q19 (the builder's cottage). But here it seems that the payment is unsolicited. In fact, respondents were not asked to assess the acceptability of this situation but instead to choose how the MP should resolve it: by returning the cheque, cashing it and donating the money to charity, or reporting the matter to the police.

The clear preference (60 per cent) was that the MP simply 'undo' the problematic act by returning the cheque (Figure 3.3).

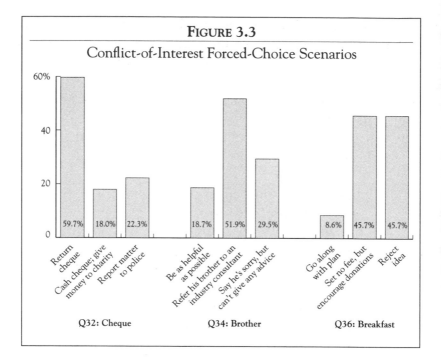

FIGURE 3.3

Conflict-of-Interest Forced-Choice Scenarios

60%

40

20

0

| 59.7% | 18.0% | 22.3% | | 18.7% | 51.9% | 29.5% | | 8.6% | 45.7% | 45.7% |

Return cheque

Cash cheque; give money to charity

Report matter to police

Be as helpful as possible

Refer his brother to an industry consultant

Say he's sorry, but can't give any advice

Go along with plan

Set no fee, but encourage donations

Reject idea

Q32: Cheque   Q34: Brother   Q36: Breakfast

This option cleanly and with no disruption returns us to a legitimate constituency service. Other respondents, however, seemed to feel that this might be like trying to put toothpaste back into the tube: is it appropriate or possible simply to pretend this attempt at a pay-off never happened? Roughly half of the remaining respondents (22 per cent) wanted the matter referred to the police, presumably not only to enable the restaurant owner's motives to be investigated, but also to ensure that there was no collusion on the part of the politician. The remaining 18 per cent preferred diverting the money to charity. The money, which would be 'dirty', if the MP kept it, is cleansed by being put to good use. On the other hand, this resolution still permits it to appear that the MP has perhaps come out ahead, if not in monetary terms (perhaps by claiming a tax credit for the donation), at least in local goodwill.

In another situation involving the most appropriate behaviour, Q34 depicts the former Energy Minister being asked by his brother, an oil company employee, for advice on whom to talk to about a tax break for his company. Again, respondents were asked to choose how the former minister should behave. Thirty per cent thought the minister could not legitimately give any assistance whatsoever without compromising the public trust. Fifty-two per cent were a bit more flexible and opted to have the minister refer his brother to an industry consultant. Both of these options remove the appearance that the minister's brother is receiving the benefit of the minister's official experience and knowledge.

The greater popularity of the referral option might be attributed to the expectation that family members will help one another as long as it does no harm. Some reject the referral because the minister may be exploiting his former contacts (even though the names of industry consultants are not restricted or privileged information). The remaining 19 per cent said the minister could be as 'helpful as possible'. While some might interpret this response as an indication that family obligations outweigh public responsibilities, it is probably due more to the very indirectness of the situation: the minister is not being asked for advice on a tax break, but simply whom to talk to about a tax break. It is reasonable to expect that some people will find this unobjectionable. The choice of response to this question is very dependent on small variations in how one regards the situation and what one sees as the salient facts in the case.

The last apparent conflict-of-interest situation concerns a cabinet minister who is trying to repay a large campaign debt (Q36). His staff proposes that he hold a $500-a-plate breakfast meeting where interested people can talk to the minister about their concerns. Fewer than 9 per cent thought that the minister should agree to this plan. These respondents were apparently untroubled by the implication that $500 might appear to buy special access to a member of cabinet. The remaining respondents were equally divided between rejecting the plan outright and—an important modification—holding the breakfast without a fixed fee, but encouraging donations (45 per cent chose each). Those who scorned the entire kaffeeklatsch concept didn't like the smell of it. They perhaps felt that it put the minister's private and political interests in conflict with his official public role. It is not the amount of money that makes the situation appear fishy, but the fact that any money at all changes hands. All constituents are supposed to have the ear of their elected officials, not just those who can pay for an appointment or even a meal.

Those who felt that the breakfast was appropriate only if the donation was voluntary may have assumed several mitigating factors. Presumably the take would be lower, and some attendees might donate a small amount or nothing at all. Of course, some might contribute far more than the proposed $500 fee, for all the possible reasons that we have discussed before. There is really only a fine line between the original plan and the donation option. In the former the minister is initiating the transaction and setting the amount; in the latter he is allowing the donor to set the price. In both instances, however, a governing official's time and attention is being set aside for those willing to pay a premium.

WHO IS MOST TOLERANT OF CONFLICTS?

No one likes conflict of interest. None of the scenarios we presented was warmly endorsed by a vast majority of respondents. However, as we have shown, Canadians do differ in some of their judgements, and, as we are about to show, these differences can be traced to crucial characteristics of the respondents.

Age: Generation X Parts Company

As mentioned in the previous chapter, we divided our sample into Generation Xers, Boomers, and Elders. Remember that the

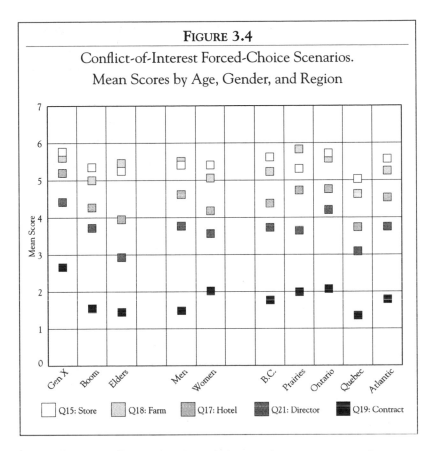

FIGURE 3.4

Conflict-of-Interest Forced-Choice Scenarios.
Mean Scores by Age, Gender, and Region

Legend: ☐ Q15: Store   ▨ Q18: Farm   ▨ Q17: Hotel   ■ Q21: Director   ■ Q19: Contract

celebrated Generation Xers are those whose economic future is often described as tenuous but who are none the less said to have abandoned guilt, duty, and fear as major motivating factors in their lives.[13] For Gen Xers, there is not much sense losing sleep over society's problems. Their egalitarian attitudes, rejection of hierarchy, and sometimes wanton permissiveness in matters of sexual relations make Gen Xers society's primary critics of traditional values. Do any of these expectations of distinctiveness translate into attitudes toward conflict of interest? And, if they do, will Gen Xers be less tolerant of conflicts of interest, given their allegedly critical attitude toward public institutions, or will

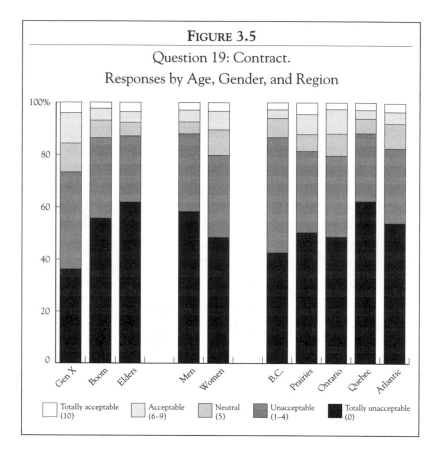

FIGURE 3.5

Question 19: Contract.

Responses by Age, Gender, and Region

Totally acceptable (10) | Acceptable (6–9) | Neutral (5) | Unacceptable (1–4) | Totally unacceptable (0)

they display the mildly anarchic, radical chic attitude of 'live and let live' often associated with youth?

It is possible, of course, that the real distinctiveness will be found at the other end of the age spectrum, among older citizens whose increasing exposure to political scandal makes them yearn for days in which politicians seemed somehow better able to chart an ethical course. Whether those days ever existed is beside the point. Older Canadians are said to be much more inclined than their younger compatriots to be certain of right and wrong in virtually every field of human endeavour.[14] They have the benefit of decades of exposure to politics and with that the

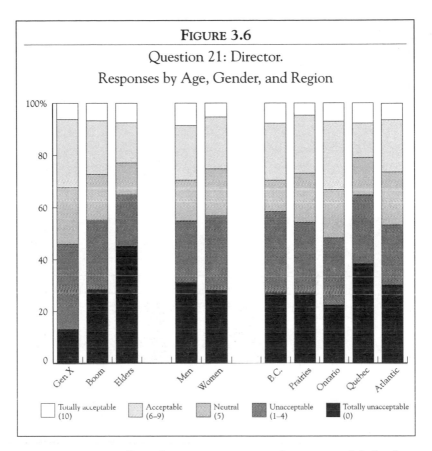

FIGURE 3.6

Question 21: Director.

Responses by Age, Gender, and Region

| □ Totally acceptable (10) | ▨ Acceptable (6–9) | ▨ Neutral (5) | ▨ Unacceptable (1–4) | ■ Totally unacceptable (0) |

opportunity to refine their expectations. It seems unlikely that many of them will have used this opportunity to lower their standards of political ethics.

Are these expectations borne out in our results? In the matter of 'actual' conflicts of interest, age does matter. Hardly anyone liked the idea of ministers accepting cottages from builders, but Generation Xers were clearly more tolerant. Compare their average response of 2.7 with the average response of 1.6 for Boomers and 1.4 for Elders (Figures 3.4 and 3.5). With most respondents clustered at the bottom of the 10-point scale, a difference of more than a point between Generation Xers and the others is

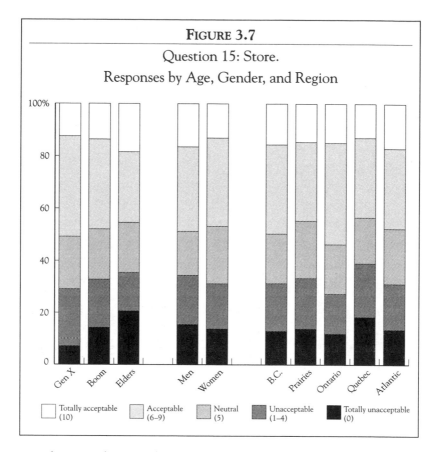

FIGURE 3.7

Question 15: Store.

Responses by Age, Gender, and Region

Legend: Totally acceptable (10) | Acceptable (6–9) | Neutral (5) | Unacceptable (1–4) | Totally unacceptable (0)

very large and certainly statistically significant. In this case, statistically different means more tolerant. The difference between Boomers and Elders, on the other hand, is relatively small.

A similar response emerges in the case of the Senator who serves as a corporate director (Figure 3.6). Once again, Generation Xers are the most tolerant, but this time Boomers and Elders are also significantly different from one another. Here we observe a clear linear relationship: the older our respondents are, the less inclined they are to accept the Senator's outside employment. This relationship breaks down, however, in the case of the store owner who votes in favour of legislation to help small business

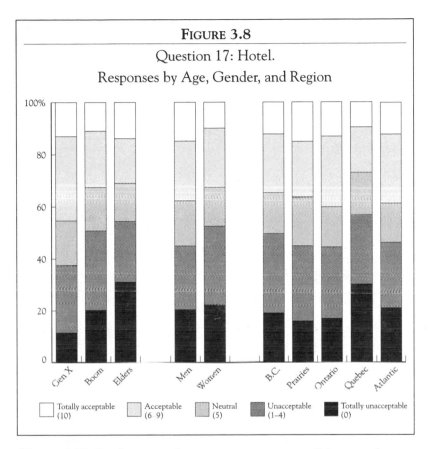

FIGURE 3.8

Question 17: Hotel.

Responses by Age, Gender, and Region

Legend:
- Totally acceptable (10)
- Acceptable (6–9)
- Neutral (5)
- Unacceptable (1–4)
- Totally unacceptable (0)

(Figure 3.7). In this case the average response is 5.4, very close to the middle of the scale, and there is no significant difference among age groups. This scenario generates a great deal of disagreement among Canadians, but very little of it can be traced to age. In sum, when it comes to 'actual' conflicts, the younger respondents stand out as more tolerant, but this applies only to the most criticized of the scenarios. Once we move to more ambiguous situations, like the store-owning MP, age doesn't matter much at all.

When we turn to 'potential' and 'apparent' conflicts of interest, the age differences reappear. The case of the hotel-owning

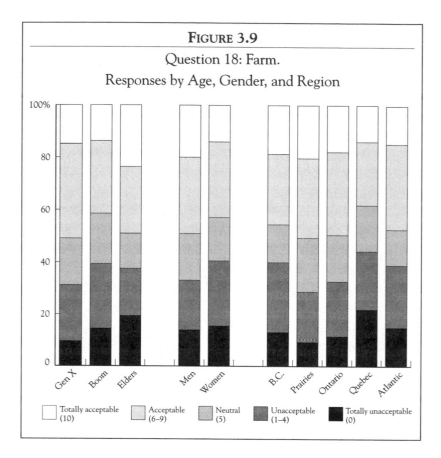

FIGURE 3.9

Question 18: Farm.

Responses by Age, Gender, and Region

cabinet minister (Q17) sees a return to the earlier pattern, with the youngest group by far the most tolerant (Figure 3.8). The average score for Gen Xers is 5.2, compared to 4.3 for Boomers and 4.0 for Elders. The case of the farm-owning Minister of Agriculture is not so simple (Figure 3.9). Recall that our respondents were less likely to criticize the farming situation (an average of 5.3 on the scale) than the hotel situation (an average of 4.4). And, as in the case of the store-owning MP, age doesn't matter as much in explaining attitudes. Generation Xers are still the most tolerant (5.6 on the scale), but Elders are close behind (5.5),

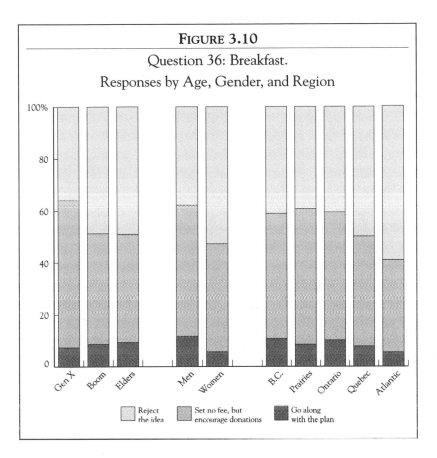

FIGURE 3.10

Question 36: Breakfast.

Responses by Age, Gender, and Region

leaving Boomers as the least tolerant (5.0). It appears that where situations are seen in a negative light in general, age matters only for how negative the attitudes are. But once there is some ambiguity about the acceptability of a scenario, age becomes a less reliable guide to attitudes.

To the extent that age matters at all, it seems to matter most for those who are in the Generation X category. The breakfast situation (Q36) provides further evidence (Figure 3.10). In this case, approximately 45 per cent of the entire sample were in favour of rejecting the whole idea. But of those in the Generation

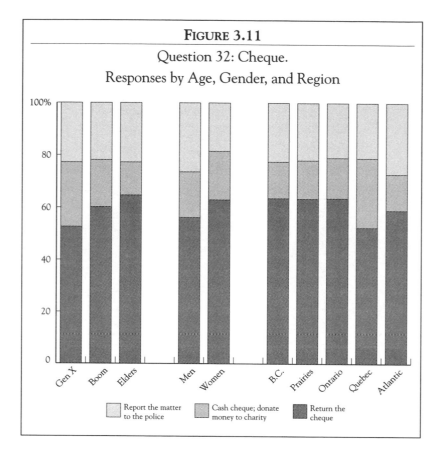

FIGURE 3.11

Question 32: Cheque.

Responses by Age, Gender, and Region

Report the matter to the police | Cash cheque; donate money to charity | Return the cheque

X category, only 36 per cent were inclined to dismiss the plan outright, whereas 49 per cent of Boomers and 50 per cent of Elders thought the idea should be rejected. Unlike their younger compatriots, Boomers and Elders were much less inclined to say that the minister should go ahead but not charge a fee. They were also less inclined to tolerate the scenario involving the MP who gets a cheque from the restaurant owner (Figure 3.11). A majority of respondents wanted him to return the cheque, but Boomers and Elders were much more inclined toward this option.

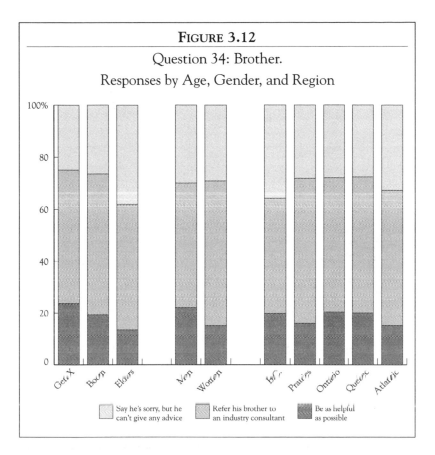

FIGURE 3.12

Question 34: Brother.

Responses by Age, Gender, and Region

There is one piece of evidence, however, that suggests that the oldest respondents may on occasion be the distinctive group. For the former minister who has to respond to his brother's request (Q34), the toughest option is to 'say he's sorry, but he can't give any advice.' Only 30 per cent of the entire sample opted for it, but among the Elders, the comparable figure was 40 per cent, and the 'be helpful' option was chosen correspondingly less often (Figure 3.12). As always, there are differences of opinion within these groups, but older Canadians are less attracted by nuanced, partial solutions to difficult problems. Yes, it would be nice for one brother to help another, but help could be misconstrued, and it would be better simply to avoid any taint of misconduct and expect the brother to understand.

Gender: Are Women Less Tolerant?

The question of whether women approach ethical choices in a manner different from men cannot be adequately answered by survey research. The results of surveys merely indicate the final product of the evaluation process, and even then the meaning attached to ultimate choices may not be the same. Carol Gilligan has argued that women construct ethical choices in a manner quite different from men, and hence are different ethical beings.[15] The results reported here show whether and where some basic differences in ultimate choices can be discerned.

Should we expect any differences? According to Michael Adams, women, true to their traditional roles as nurturers, are more inclined to be pro-environment and opposed to cruelty to animals. And they are much more inclined to support multiculturalism and alternative family structures.[16] They tend to be more sceptical than men of the ability of the market economy to resolve society's problems, and to be more approving of social programs.[17] But are women more or less tolerant when it comes to political ethics? Does a propensity to be nurturing lead women to be more forgiving about transgressions, or do women feel more alienated from politics with the result that they are inclined to criticize the behaviour of a male-dominated political elite?

As it happens, basic differences are not always obvious in our survey, and when they occur, they are rather perplexing. Take, for example, the instances of 'actual' conflict we have identified. Men and women have virtually identical attitudes toward the Senator who serves as a corporate director (Q21). This is not an easy case and there is much division of opinion, but that division is not reflected on gender grounds.

Women and men do not agree when it comes to obvious cases. In the case of the minister who accepts the cottage (Q19), almost everyone finds this conduct unacceptable, but women are less damning in their judgement. In the cases of potential conflict, the positions are reversed. Women are more inclined to the 'unacceptable' end of the spectrum in both cases, and although the differences are statistically significant, they are rather small in terms of the whole scale.

As for 'apparent conflict', our case of the store-owning MP who votes for legislation helpful to small business (Q15) results in no appreciable differences at all between men and women. On this item men and women are virtually identical in their responses, in spite of great disarray in the overall pattern of answers to this question. But women are more uneasy than men about the former minister who is approached by his brother looking for advice. Here 43 per cent of women suggest that the former minister should be helpful; 57 per cent of men choose this option.

In short, gender differences exist, but they are small and inconsistent. That is, it is not possible to say that either men or women are always more tolerant of conflict of interest.

The Impact of Region: Quebec Stands Out

Regional differences are not large, but they are consistent. When residents of different parts of the country differ in assessing conflict of interest, Quebeckers almost invariably establish a tougher standard. For example, Quebeckers are the least tolerant of the Minister of Tourism who owns a large hotel and of the Minister of Agriculture who owns a large farm. Quebeckers are the least forgiving of the Senator who serves as a corporate director and the minister who accepts the free use of a cottage. The differences are not large, and Quebeckers do not always distinguish themselves from respondents in every other region. But they are consistently the least tolerant of these situations. The results are almost always statistically significant, and there are no statistically significant differences that involve regions other than Quebec. The only departures from this pattern occur in the forced-choice questions. In the case of the restaurant owner who sent his MP the unsolicited cheque, Quebeckers are more inclined than those living elsewhere in Canada to suggest that the cheque be cashed and the money donated to charity. In the matter of the breakfast club, Quebeckers resemble all others, and it is those from Atlantic Canada who are distinctive. Whereas fewer than 50 per cent of respondents in all of the other regions suggest that the minister reject the idea of a private breakfast to raise funds (only 39 per cent of Prairie respondents thought this was the best idea), 59 per cent of respondents living in Atlantic Canada rejected it outright. This is the only instance in which Quebeckers did not follow a separate, narrower path.

The traditional view that Quebeckers are more tolerant of compromising situations receives no support in the data. Although regional differences are not pronounced, where they do occur, Quebeckers usually are less tolerant than others.

CONCLUSION

We began by observing that conflicts of interest happen when the responsibilities associated with our different roles are incompatible with one another. In the particular situations we have examined, Canadians told us what they think about these situations and efforts to resolve the conflicts. Very few found any of the conflict scenarios acceptable. There is a strong judgemental streak running through the responses, with only the most innocuous of situations gaining any kind of acceptance whatsoever. Conflict of interest seems to be palatable only when the conflict is not direct but rather more oblique, such as when the politician's private interest turns out to be widely shared, so that even if he does act in his own benefit, many other private citizens are likely to benefit as well. The interest promoted in the case of the farm and the clothing store is still not the true public interest, but it is at least not entirely that of the politician involved.

That said, it must be acknowledged that our respondents were prepared to make distinctions. They were very severe about outright conflicts and more tolerant of potential and apparent conflicts. And when it came to resolving them, the people we sampled differed among themselves about the best way of handling the situation. We traced these differences to several background variables, particularly age. So-called Generation Xers proved to be a distinctive group, both more tolerant of the conflicts themselves and more inclined to choose different means for resolving them. Gender and region matter as well, but these differences were less pronounced.

One of the situations we discussed involved an outright gift as part of a conflict situation. Gifts in a political context are not, however, always indicative of conflict of interest. In the next chapter we examine gifts in and of themselves, as well as some special gifts that come with the office. It will be interesting to see whether the patterns we have discovered so far persist.

Patrick Corrigan cartoon from *The Toronto Star*, 19 April 1996.
Reprinted with permission - The Toronto Star Syndicate.

Chapter Four

GIFTS
AND GAINS

In idealistic circles, political office is thought of as a noble calling: not just a job, but an adventure in public service. Nevertheless, those who heed the call end up with a salary that is quite a bit higher than the national average. The scandals splashed across today's newspapers and TV news reports reveal a continued journalistic fascination with tales of elected officials' involvement with 'gifts' and 'gains', the perquisites that come with holding public office. As Edmund Burke, one of the foremost parliamentarians of the eighteenth century, pointed out, elected officials can't be expected to take an oath of poverty in the name of 'serving the public'.[1] If they were, why would anyone run for political office? But neither do citizens of modern democracies expect politicians to use their offices to extract personal gains or to seek out gifts in the course of undertaking their public duties.

It would appear, however, that these are very popular perceptions of political reality. Fuelled by a seemingly endless litany of stories about cars and drivers, trips abroad to exotic locales, the frivolous use of government airplanes, splendid offices, and bottomless expense accounts—public contempt has snowballed for politicians who seem unwilling to see that the favours they grant themselves are considered excessive and resented by many.[2] Private citizens affected harshly by high unemployment and corporate downsizing were naturally cynical when Senator Andrew Thompson continued to draw his $64,000 salary while never showing up for work, or for that matter even leaving his Mexican villa, where, he said, his medical problems kept him house-bound.[3] Voters hard-pressed to pay their mortgages were pertur-bed when Reform Party Leader Preston Manning, claiming to be simply following the wave of public sentiment, moved into Storn-oway, the house provided at public expense to the Leader of the Official Opposition, and the very house he had denounced as an intolerably wasteful extravagance when it was not his to refuse.[4]

While these images of largesse and excess abound, it is important to note that the perks of politics are not as lavish as the public might think. In recent years, Ottawa has taken steps to reduce and eliminate some of the extras accruing to members of the political elite. An MP's salary pales in comparison to the income of corporate executives, though it remains a good one. (MPs are paid a salary of $64,400 a year and also receive a tax-free expense allowance of $21,300, which they do not have to account for with receipts.[5]) They receive generous travel entitle-ments that can be used for themselves, their spouses, dependent children, and staff. In 1992, first-class travel was eliminated, although business class airfare is still allowed.

Parliament Hill offices come well-equipped (although furni-ture allowances for constituency offices were eliminated in June 1997), and our representatives have access to free postal service, long distance calls, messenger services, museums, tours, day care, and a tailor. Today, however, members must pay to use the gym-nasium, barber or hairdresser, and masseur. Though meals can still be taken at the parliamentary dining room, the prices have been raised to nearly those of commercial restaurants. And the much envied parliamentary pension scheme was made less gen-erous by Prime Minister Chrétien in 1995. The new system scaled back benefits by about 25 per cent, and members have to wait until age 55 to collect. Previously, retiring or defeated MPs could begin collecting pensions as soon as they left office. However, pension credits are still earned at a rate of 4 per cent a year compared to 2 per cent in most private plans, and a member has only to serve six years in order to qualify.

So why is it that although cuts have been made to the perks of public office, perceptions of abuse persist? Part of the explanation must be the politicization of these perks by the media and politicians themselves. The National Citizens Coalition has conducted several successful campaigns against what it sees as excessive spending by the government on its own members. Increasingly, members of one party have been only too willing to allege abuse by members of another, in order to score points with the electorate.

Like powerful executives, politicians are in a position to attract a lot of attention from those who may gain or lose from their decisions, attention that can be demonstrated with a little something now and then. Gifts that are large and come with obvious strings attached have a special name—'bribes'—and they have a special section in the Criminal Code as well. There is very little confusion or disagreement about the unacceptability of bribery. But what about a thank-you card, a souvenir pen, a bottle of wine, or a couple of hockey tickets? Banks and department store perfume counters offer all of us 'free gifts' when we choose to do business with them; is the same practice acceptable for public officials? At what point does a token of gratitude or generosity start to represent one side of a mutual obligation?

Gifts are just as much grist for the scandal mill as outrageous perks. The Liberal and NDP opposition made quite a fuss over the leaked news that Ontario Premier Mike Harris's riding association was footing his membership dues at two exclusive golf and country clubs. A few years earlier, as an opposition leader, Harris had joined in attacking NDP member Tony Rizzo for accepting free blueprints from an architect who later won a government contract. Governments can also attract attention as the source of gifts, as did Nova Scotia in 1994, when it tried to dispose of 'slow mover' souvenirs in a pre-Christmas half-off sale. And of course there are some gifts that, in the end, work out ideally for all concerned: how would the Chrétiens have defended themselves from an intruder at 24 Sussex without a handy (and heavy) Inuit carving that had been presented to the Prime Minister?

Of course, part of the frustration of following politics is that the same 'sky-is-falling' indignant rhetoric that characterizes campaign speeches about the multi-billion dollar Pearson Airport deal is used in asking who paid for a few of Preston Manning's suits. The key to sorting out what is acceptable and what is not is to understand the activities themselves and the circumstances involved. By virtue of their public office, politicians are in position to receive certain benefits denied to ordinary citizens. We divide these benefits into 'gifts' and 'gains'.

Defining 'Gifts' and 'Gains'

Everybody loves to receive gifts. Whether on your birthday, at Christmas, other special occasions, or just for no reason at all. Gifts necessarily involve an exchange relationship: there is a giver and a receiver. Undoubtedly, there are a whole range of circumstances where the giving and receiving of gifts is an entirely innocent transaction. At the end of a hotel stay, for example, it is not unusual for a satisfied guest to leave a gratuity for the person who did a good job cleaning the room. Fair enough. Most people view this sort of exchange, a 'tip', as nothing more than a thoughtful expression of gratitude and generosity.

It is unlikely that the person on the receiving end of the tip will be in any position to have a profound effect on the fortunes of the giver. It is hardly plausible that such a tip could provide the springboard for any unethical 'future considerations' or some sort of underhanded mutual backscratching. None the less, at the other end of the scale, there are obviously cases where a gift is nothing short of an outright bribe. It may be explicit: you do this for me, and I will pay you $500. Turned upside down, this is known as extortion: if you don't do this for me, I will find ways to punish you. But the transaction can also be far more subtle, involving some sort of implicit bargain, an unspoken but shared expectation about future considerations. Mutually understood arrangements have been proposed with a sidelong glance and sealed with nothing more than a wink.

In the political realm, gifts can take many forms. Cash is not the only medium. Hospitality, such as a meal or hotel stay, or free travel to some desirable locale—the infamous 'junket'—are common ways in which appreciation can be shown or obligations imposed. Officials may be given gifts 'in kind', that is, items of value that have some relation to a function or visit. Of course the higher the value and the less closely related the gift, the more eyebrows are raised. Gifts may come after some other act, as a gesture of thanks, or before, as a gesture of hope for future consideration. When they exceed our standards of propriety, these are known respectively as 'pay-offs' and 'bribes'.

Politicians are also often the givers of what seem like lavish presents, such as contracts to supporters, ambassadorships to defeated MPs, new government offices to ministers' ridings, and so on. To many, these acts are a form of gift, but political scientists think such exchanges are so interesting they give them the special name of 'patronage'. The next chapter of this book is devoted to this time-honoured political activity, but this one is concerned only with gifts received by public officials.

We distinguish gifts from gains by the absence of a particular identifiable giver. Gains are the perks, benefits, and special deals that officials receive only because of their political position. In a sense, a gain is a present from the government or the public purse itself, rather than from some other player in the political game. In this definition of gains, the 'undeserved' connotation of 'gift' is also strong: they are 'extras', not something one is necessarily entitled to, but never the less obtained. Realistically, it is hardly surprising that the people we choose to make the rules in our society should create at least some benefits for themselves, such as generous pensions, subsidized meals, and chauffeured limousines. But not all gains are necessarily acceptable or legal, and some politicians, perhaps unsatisfied with their ordinary perks, have shown great creativity in bending the rules to increase their benefits. A modest expense account is a gain, but one that most of us would find reasonable given the demands of politics. A manipulated and inflated expense account is a gain of a different sort.

With political gifts, the big question is usually 'why?' Why is this gift being given? What are the expectations of the giver? With gains, we already know why: gains are incentives or compensation for the demands of a complex and relatively low-paying job. The question that arises is then 'how much?' or 'how much is too much?'

DEFENDING GIFTS AND GAINS

Gifts given to politicians in the course of discharging their public responsibilities are complicated. Unlike gifts received from relatives and friends, these gifts are given to the politicians because of their position. How do you decide what to do with such a gift? Politicians find it difficult to refuse gifts, especially from grateful constituents. How can they refuse a token of appreciation without causing insult and hurting the giver's feelings? Often these gifts may be presented at a public ceremony and the politician has little choice but to accept what is being offered. So the first argument that can be advanced in defence of accepting a gift is one of courtesy. To refuse would be considered rude or offensive.

Gifts are Harmless Tokens of Courtesy

In part there is a cultural argument to be made here. In some countries it is expected that gifts will be given as expressions of gratitude to representatives who help out in a personal way, or on a special occasion, or at the end of a speech to a group or organization. The giving of gifts is viewed as natural and the right thing to do. To turn the gift down might do more harm than good, and by refusing, the politician might very well offend supporters. In addition, the gifts that are usually offered in such situations are not extravagant. They tend to be tokens, small items intended to convey a sentiment. They are often hand-made crafts or art works, or homemade products, gifts that have no commercial value.

When gifts start to get expensive, however, this kind of explanation loses most of its persuasiveness. For example, in the course of his many foreign trips, Prime Minister Mulroney received numerous valuable gifts from foreign leaders. Some were in return for ones he had given on behalf of the people of Canada. An expensive example is the $1½ million Canadian painting that Mulroney gave to France during the bicentennial of the French Revolution. What few people realize is that when he left office Mulroney kept thousands of dollars worth of gifts that had been presented to him, including an ancient Roman cup given to him by Israel, a replica of the Gutenberg Bible from France, and an antique pot and clock from the Aga Khan.[6] These were given to the leader of Canada, and Brian Mulroney would not have received them if he had not been our Prime Minister. Should these objects have remained in the official residence of the Prime Minister, or been donated to a public gallery so that all might enjoy and appreciate them?

If it is improper to accept gifts and rude to refuse them, what is a politician to do? One possible solution is to accept the gifts and display them in the member's constituency office. Another is to raffle the gift off and donate the proceeds to charity in the name of the giver of the gift. Or the gift could be distributed among or shared with the member's staff, assuming that is possible. Or, since politicians are also expected to give gifts, what is received on one occasion could be given away on another (with care to avoid recycling a gift to the wrong person). There are a number of ways to ensure that the gift is not seen to be the personal property of the elected official. Part of the problem is that at the federal level the nature and value of gifts are not made public. The most recently proposed (but abandoned) code of conduct for parliamentarians would have required MPs to register gifts worth $250 or more in the member's annual declaration form (which would have been a public document) and to indicate the source of the gift and the approximate value.

Gains Keep Qualified People in the Public Sector

We often hear that gains are necessary to offset the costs of public office. Politicians contend that the burdens of public office are costly both to themselves and to their families, and so their job, not unlike other jobs, comes with certain 'gains' that help make the job more palatable. To make up for a salary that by business standards is inadequate, a tax-free expense account is only sensible. To shorten the time spent away from one's family, free air travel seems perfectly reasonable. And, in view of the size of the country, so too does free long distance telephone service.

The fact is, politicians do have demanding jobs. Free travel sounds cushy, but flying constantly back and forth between Vancouver and Ottawa soon loses its glamour. Maintaining an office, staff, and living quarters in two locations is something rarely required outside the upper echelons of the corporate world, where of course the salaries are usually padded to compensate for such inconvenience. While many ridiculed Chrétien's observation that even he took home less than the lowest-paid NHL player, he at least produced a balanced budget in 1998; the Canadian NHLers couldn't buy a medal at the Nagano Olympics.

It is in everyone's interest to keep parliamentary salaries and benefits somewhat competitive with what the same people could earn elsewhere. Since we inevitably grant MPs a great deal of responsibility, we want to be able to recruit and keep qualified candidates. We have all invested in Canada, and we all need a strong cabinet that will keep generating strong dividends for the country's citizens. But we don't want our investment wasted on lavish executive parties, padded expense accounts, and overly generous pension plans.

Gains Are an Ordinary Business Practice

The amenities package offered to politicians is like those that come as part of many employment packages. And its beneficiaries would argue that it is certainly not as generous as those offered to the CEOs of large Canadian corporations. To make up for the apparent deficiencies, political parties and riding associations are more and more often picking up the tab for items like a Hawaiin vacation for the Mannings or new suits for Mike Harris. These types of gains also provide lucrative tax credits for the political donors. But as Liberal MP Ethel Blondin-Andrew discovered, the acceptability of such gains does not extend to using a government credit card to buy a fur coat and a vacation, even if you intend to reimburse the expense account for the charges.[7]

Complicating all of this is the fact that the government guidelines, at least for federal MPs, don't cover every possible situation or every type of gift, nor indeed could they. Codes of conduct vary from province to province, and even in provinces with well-developed codes, the restrictions on gifts and whether they must be declared or registered or foregone depend on the gift itself and the circumstances. More than that, all of these codes and guidelines are constantly evolving.

The fact that the codes are uneven, that standards apply to some people but not others, and that the targets are moving does not necessarily mean that there are no ethical standards at all. By what standards, though, do you know when something is improper? According to Dennis Thompson, it is not the motive that matters here. Nor is it the gain itself, or even the benefit. The real criterion is whether the connection between the gain and the benefit 'damages the democratic process'.[8] Thompson's notion of the unethical fine-tunes the conventional standards by adding what he calls 'an appearance standard'. In everyday language this might be better called a 'smell test'. And in democracies the arbiter of this smell test is the public nose.

So what kinds of gifts and gains do citizens find acceptable and unacceptable? Where do members of our sample draw the line? To what extent is there agreement about the acceptability or unacceptability of accepting gifts? And under what circumstances do people think it is all right for elected representatives to accept gifts or receive a gain? Our survey used a variety of means to probe these issues, to get a sense of where Canadians detect a mere whiff of the unethical, where they are overpowered by its pungency, and where and when elected officials come up roses.

CANADIANS EVALUATE GIFTS AND GAINS

To begin, members of the sample were asked two questions about gifts and gains that were somewhat more personal. Specifically, they were asked to decide whether they found the following activities usually, sometimes, rarely, or never acceptable. The first (Q6d), 'accepting a gift for doing your job', was judged to be acceptable (usually or sometimes) by about 65 per cent of our sample, while 12 per cent said it was 'rarely' acceptable and 24 per cent chose 'never' (Figure 4.1). In other words, most people seemed to think this was all right. Note that many companies forbid this kind of gratuity, as anyone knows who has tried to tip a flight attendant. When it comes to 'claiming benefits you are not entitled to' (Q6f), the respondents were not nearly as tolerant. Almost 85 per cent deemed this to be 'never' acceptable.

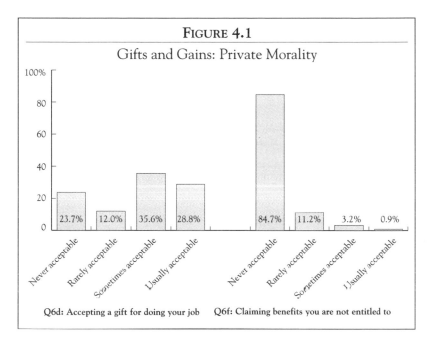

FIGURE 4.1

Gifts and Gains: Private Morality

Q6d: Accepting a gift for doing your job   Q6f: Claiming benefits you are not entitled to

Only about 3 per cent scored it acceptable.

The difference between the response to the two questions may be attributed to the fact that the benefits question implies the cheating of a system to which everyone contributes. By claiming something that you are not entitled to, you are depleting the system more quickly and depriving someone of assistance who may truly need it. It would seem that at least in their own private lives, respondents are very understanding about gifts but less so about exploiting the system. This suggests a possible generalization, namely, that Canadians prefer gifts to gains. Let's see whether this holds in the evaluation of politicians.

Gifts

The first scenario deals with the case of an expensive gift: 'On a trip to the Northwest Territories, a cabinet minister meets with a group of local artists who present him with a valuable carving.

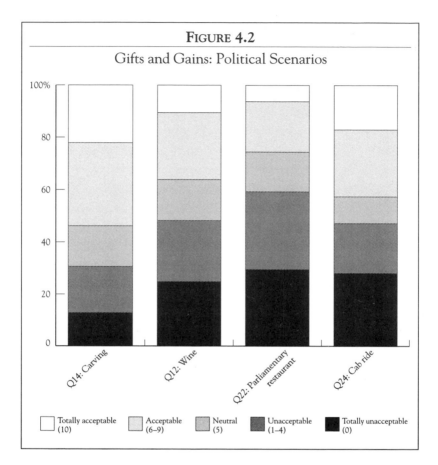

FIGURE 4.2

Gifts and Gains: Political Scenarios

Legend:
Totally acceptable (10) | Acceptable (6–9) | Neutral (5) | Unacceptable (1–4) | Totally unacceptable (0)

Chart categories: Q14: Carving | Q12: Wine | Q22: Parliamentary restaurant | Q24: Cab ride

On his return, he displays the carving in his home' (Q14). The response to this question is quite divided: 54 per cent find it acceptable for the minister to accept the gift, but 31 per cent think it is unacceptable (Figure 4.2). How can we account for this difference in opinion? Nothing in the wording of the scenario implies that any ministerial promises have been made to do something special for the group of artists. Nor is there any indication that the cabinet minister has in any way been compromised by the exchange. None the less, the fact remains that the carving is described as valuable, which may have led people to decide that this particular exchange involves something more than a mere token.

Most governments have guidelines about disclosing to the government's ethics office any gifts that exceed a value of $200 to $250. But this technicality is not really the issue. There are deeper questions lurking around this transaction. Does the exchange qualify as a courtesy? And if it is first and foremost a matter of courtesy, is it realistic to suppose that the minister in question can say 'thanks but no thanks' without trampling the sensitivities of the artists? Then again, the minister is surely not personally responsible for the fact that the carving in question turns out to be valuable. How likely is it that a group of artists deliberately set out to unload a bad piece of art on a visiting dignitary? However, those who scored it unacceptable may be reasoning that the minister does benefit personally from the transaction by being able to enjoy the art, not in a public place like a museum, a library, a school, or even his parliamentary office, but at home. Moreover, was the gift a 'thank-you' to the minister as a person, or to him in his role as government official? Displaying the gift at home implies the recipient deems it personal property; displaying it in the office would connect it more directly with an official function.

More than three-quarters of the respondents thought that people in politics frequently accept gifts like this; only 14 per cent said otherwise. It seems that people are inclined to think that this kind of gift giving goes on all the time. The general approval of this gift is in keeping with the basic acceptance of gifts, previously noted in private life. In this area, respondents appear to be consistent in their evaluations.

The other gift question that was posed, however, contradicts this conclusion. Q12 reads: 'At Christmas, a Member of Parliament accepts a bottle of wine from a constituent who is grateful for help in speeding up the paperwork to get a passport.' This act was unacceptable for 48 per cent, including 25 per cent who found it totally unacceptable. Thirty-seven per cent found it acceptable. This scenario may also be viewed as an example of accepting a gift for doing your job, even though MPs are expected to perform this kind of service for their constituents without a special reward (other than re-election). Unlike the carving, which is a public, ceremonial, and symbolic gift from an artists' group, this bottle of wine is practically a tip. We accept tips as reasonable recompense for low-paid, low-status service jobs, and we assume that the expectation of a good tip results in attentive service. But this is not the sort of behaviour most citizens would expect from their elected representatives.

On the other hand, a single bottle of wine pales in comparison to some gifts that politicians have received, such as the 20-odd pounds of beef, blueberries, and strawberries, tickets to the Grey Cup, and liquor that two Ontario cabinet ministers were alleged to have received in exchange for assistance in obtaining a trucking licence from the Ontario Highway Transport Board.[9] Some respondents may have considered a single bottle of wine to be a harmless gesture—a slightly more expensive version of a thank-you card, and not something that could be seen as compromising an MP's integrity or judgement. Besides, since the gift came after the passport was obtained, the wine was not a requirement for assistance. In this light it is somewhat surprising that so many people found this expression of appreciation unacceptable. Perhaps they were being particularly sensitive to the appearance of favouritism that is created by the giving (and accepting) of gifts. Recall our findings in the previous chapter on the matter of appearance.

Gains

Three scenarios are relevant to the discussion of gains. Question 22 concerns an MP who uses the parliamentary restaurant, where the prices are subsidized, to host dinners for visiting constituents.

Fifty-nine per cent of the respondents found this unacceptable, including nearly 30 per cent who said it was totally unacceptable, compared to the 26 per cent who found it acceptable (Figure 4.2). That parliamentarians have a restaurant to call their own is surely a perk. But that is not unusual, and there are quite practical reasons for such an arrangement since MPs work long and sometimes inconvenient hours. Moreover, in Ottawa, the Parliament Buildings are some distance from public restaurants, and on those grounds alone it may make sense for elected officials to have some eating facilities on hand. But should the MPs' own restaurant be subsidized? The idea that MPs are 'up there on the hill getting a free meal at public expense' is unlikely to generate much public sympathy, particularly during times of financial restraint. Still, most of the activities of the House are subsidized in one way or another, and it can be argued that there are parallels in the private sector, where business lunches and dinners are subsidized in the sense that they can be written off as expenses. A tax deduction for business meals effectively means that we are all helping to pay for them.

That the restaurant is being used to host a dinner for visiting constituents is surely a complication. Presumably some of our respondents may have pictured themselves on the receiving end of the *hors d'oeuvre* platter. If the taxpayers are paying to help subsidize the restaurant, why shouldn't they reap the benefits when they are visiting the Hill? But the results do not support this perspective; they also indicate that nearly 80 per cent of respondents thought that people in politics frequently do this kind of thing. So it would seem that the popular perception is that wining and dining at public expense is commonplace but that engaging in it is bad form for everyone, including constituents.

The second gains scenario (Q24) is about workplace practices: 'After working late on constituency business, an MP takes a cab home and charges it to the government'. This time respondents were more evenly divided in their response. While 47 per cent of respondents found this unacceptable (28 per cent totally), 43 per cent found it acceptable. What is at issue here? This is a perk, true, but not a particularly unusual one. There are no codified government provisions that explicitly prohibit the use of a cab; in fact there are fairly routine arrangements made for people who work overtime to charge the cab 'to the office'. Moreover, people who are in the private sector may reasonably expect to get such a perk if they worked late at the office. The value of this perk is trivial by any standard.

The sticking point here may be that the cost of this perk is explicitly attached to the public purse; the cab is charged 'to the government'. Notice the implict double standard at the core of this explanation. An act that would go without comment (and certainly without criticism) in the private sector is considered by almost half of our respondents to be unacceptable in the public realm. Obviously, some people need to ask themselves just why public officials should have to spend their own money to do their jobs when those in the private sector do not.

The final gain question revolves around a cabinet minister who must attend an important meeting in Europe. 'He is issued a first-class plane ticket. His wife who sees very little of her husband would like to go along' (Q38). Respondents were asked what they thought the minister should do. Should the minister: a) take his wife along at his own expense; b) trade in his first-class fare for two seats in economy; or c) go alone? A majority of the respondents, 64 per cent, thought that the minister should personally pay for his wife's ticket (Figure 4.3). Twenty-seven per cent went for the trade-in scheme, and interestingly enough, only 8 per cent thought the minister should go alone. What the results seem to indicate is some sympathy for the position of political spouse. People may have felt that politics is a heavy burden on a marriage and that the wife should be permitted to accompany her husband.

The big question is 'at whose expense', and the majority

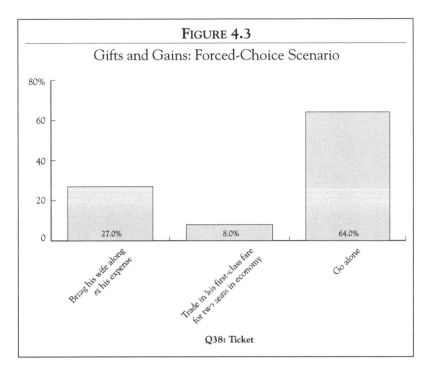

FIGURE 4.3

Gifts and Gains: Forced-Choice Scenario

80%

60

40

20

0

27.0%   8.0%   64.0%

Bring his wife along at his expense

Trade in his first-class fare for two seats in economy

Go alone

Q38: Ticket

think it should be the minister's. While the trade-in option was popular, people may think that the politician should be travelling in first class, whether from a status point of view, or in order to ensure that he arrives at his destination relaxed and ready to conduct government business. If he doesn't want to enjoy the more comfortable seat, he should save the government some money by downgrading, but he shouldn't effectively pocket the difference in fare. And for those who said the minister should go alone, perhaps the importance of the meeting seemed to suggest that he wouldn't have very much time for his wife anyway and she might even become a distraction.

Overall, it seems fair to say that Canadians are consistently more tolerant of gifts than they are of gains, in both public and private life. This is not a hard and fast rule—certainly we would have found somewhat different results if we had asked about more blatant gifts like a new car or a major appliance. But the contrast between the two scenarios is instructive. Even though it is hard to imagine that a cab ride would cost anything close to the value of a piece of Inuit art, the respondents were more critical of the free ride than the free gift. Moreover, since the official has apparently put in some overtime at personal inconvenience, it could be that the government benefits from arranging to pay for the cab. No such case can be made that keeping the carving at home results in a net gain for the public. One possibility is that the gift is seen as essentially personal and therefore questions of value do not pertain. On the other hand, perhaps the respondents feel that officials do not deserve any more perks, even small ones, because they are already too well taken care of. Finally we note that gifts of travel are one area where there are explicit rules (sponsored foreign travel must be declared by MPs), but travel gains are perhaps particularly identified with excess in the public mind because government junkets and expense accounts are often pulled out as examples of profligacy and waste.

WHO TOLERATES GIFTS AND GAINS?

As with conflict of interest, no one was particularly charitable about political gifts and gains. But previous work in this field and the findings presented in the last chapter suggest that we should still expect different segments of the sample to react in different ways to the scenarios. Where are the irregularities in this part of the ethical map?

Age: Gaining Age and the Gift of Wisdom?

The clearest pattern that emerged in the data as a whole was that once again Generation Xers stood apart from the rest, and that, for the most part, tolerance decreased with age. This was espe-

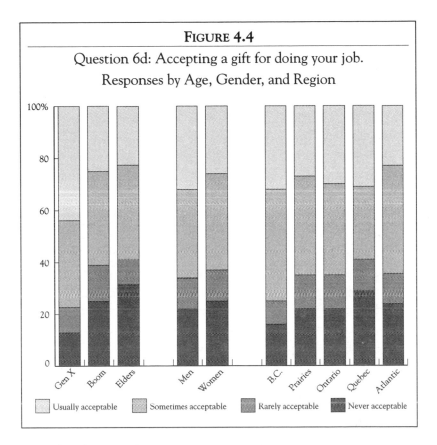

FIGURE 4.4

Question 6d: Accepting a gift for doing your job.
Responses by Age, Gender, and Region

Usually acceptable Sometimes acceptable Rarely acceptable Never acceptable

cially evident with respect to the 'things people do', the area of personal ethical judgement. Thirty-two per cent of Elders deemed it never acceptable to accept a gift for doing your job (Q6d), and only 22 per cent thought it usually acceptable (Figure 4.4). Among Generation Xers, only 13 per cent chose never, and 43 per cent felt it was usually acceptable. Few respondents of any age thought it was ever acceptable to claim benefits to which one is not entitled, but almost one in four Xers chose rarely, sometimes, or usually on Q6f; fewer than one in 10 Elders selected anything other than never (Figure 4.5). In both cases, the Boomers firmly occupied the middle ground. This certainly does

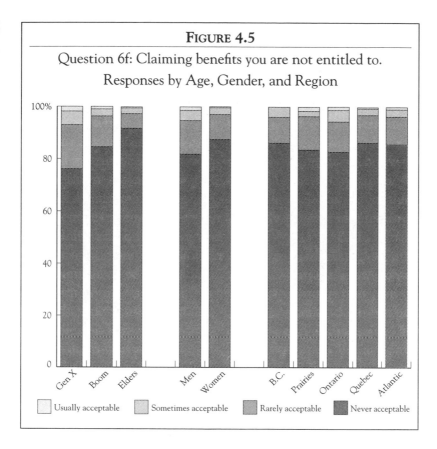

FIGURE 4.5

Question 6f: Claiming benefits you are not entitled to.
Responses by Age, Gender, and Region

little to refute the generational accusation that 'kids today want something for nothing'.

Generation Xers were also significantly less critical of situations like the carving, the use of the restaurant, and the bottle of wine (Figures 4.6 to 4.9). This difference was somewhat less pronounced in the latter two scenarios; in those it was the Elders who were distinctive by their relative intolerance. The same general pattern applied to the minister flying to Europe (Figure 4.10); Xers were more likely to suggest that he exchange the ticket, Elders preferred that he pay his wife's way. Boomers stood out by their reluctance to choose the 'leave his wife at home'

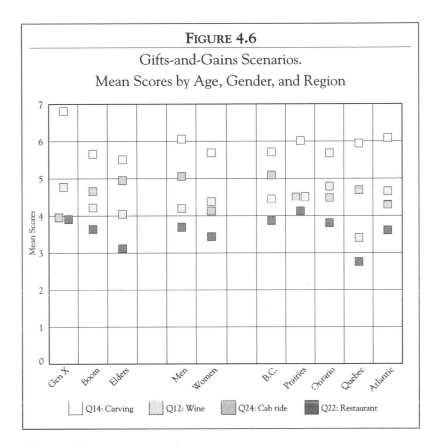

FIGURE 4.6

Gifts-and-Gains Scenarios.

Mean Scores by Age, Gender, and Region

☐ Q14: Carving   ▨ Q12: Wine   ▨ Q24: Cab ride   ■ Q22: Restaurant

option. Perhaps the vaunted popularity of cocooning amongst Boomers is behind this tendency. If you have to leave the family hearth, do what you can to take it with you.

The striking exception to this trend was the cab ride charged to the government. Generation Xers were strongly and significantly more critical of this item than the rest of the sample (Figure 4.11). This may be due to differences in familiarity with such perks: those under 30 tend to be on the lower rungs of the career ladder, where such advantages are not available and are perhaps resented. This stance jibes with the sceptical, anti-hierarchical mood of Gen Xers, who question the legitimacy of someone's getting a special deal. But if that is the explanation, why have they been more tolerant of all the other scenarios so far? There may be something about this particular situation, perhaps its trivial banality, that serves as a focus for criticism. Of all the scenarios in the questionnaire, this is the one that a private citizen is most likely to experience firsthand.

Gender: Gifts 'n' Gains 'n' Guys 'n' Gals 'n' Buttons 'n' Bows

In evaluations of private ethical choices, there is some evidence of variation between men and women. Men were more likely to hedge on claiming benefits; women were more categorical. Lower female tolerance was also weakly apparent in connection with the job-related gift. All told, however, the gender gap is fairly narrow in the area of private gifts and gains.

When we turn to politics, two scenarios did not even display a hairline fracture: the gift of wine and the dinner at the parliamentary restaurant were evaluated in much the same way by men and women. But women tended to view the other three situations in a harsher light. Once again, familiarity with perks seems a plausible explanation, for the gender gap widened consistently from Generation X to the Elders. Young men and women were essentially indistinguishable in their opinions about the cab ride, for example (their average responses are both 3.9 out of 10), but Elder women (4.2) were significantly more critical than Elder men (5.9). The mass participation in the workforce by women is a phenomenon that many Elder women missed. Just as demographic constraints have retarded the advancement of Gen Xers to the perk-rich upper echelons of employment, cultural factors and the 'glass ceiling' have kept women of all ages from enjoying many of the good things that the 'boys' network' accumulates for itself.

Women were also more likely to insist that the minister take his wife along at his own expense, rather than trade in his ticket

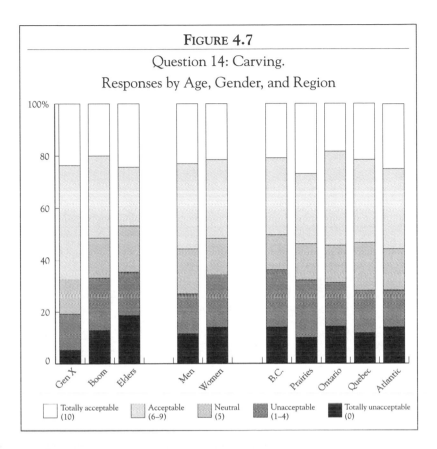

FIGURE 4.7

Question 14: Carving.

Responses by Age, Gender, and Region

Legend:
Totally acceptable (10) | Acceptable (6–9) | Neutral (5) | Unacceptable (1–4) | Totally unacceptable (0)

or leave her at home. This reveals not only sympathy for the wife's desire to travel with her husband, but also an insistence that it be done above board.

Region: Souvenirs of Your Trip To...

We found no strong differences among the regions in answers to the questions about the 'things people do'. Certainly when it comes to claiming undeserved benefits, Canadians across the country are uniformly intolerant. As far as gifts are concerned, Quebeckers are somewhat distinctive, not for any particular

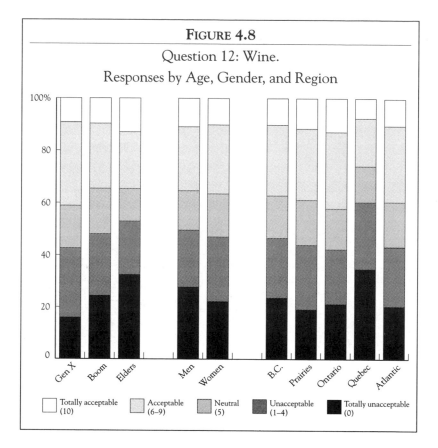

FIGURE 4.8

Question 12: Wine.

Responses by Age, Gender, and Region

tendency, but for the polarization of their responses. Somewhat more so than in other provinces, Quebeckers tended to deem accepting a gift for doing your job either never acceptable or usually acceptable; the middle ground was depleted.

The only significant regional variation apparent in the political scenarios was that Quebeckers were much more critical than non-Quebeckers of the gift of wine and the use of the subsidized parliamentary restaurant. Interestingly enough, these two 'consumable' gifts and gains were precisely those which men and women evaluated in essentially the same manner.

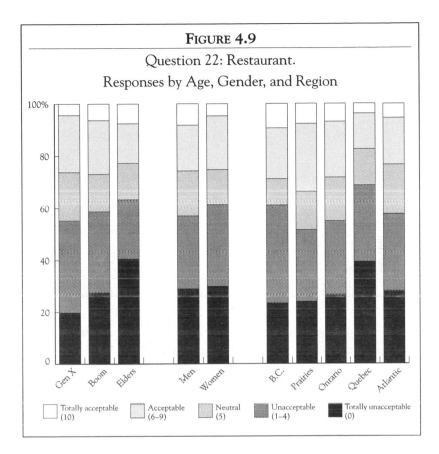

FIGURE 4.9

Question 22: Restaurant.

Responses by Age, Gender, and Region

Totally acceptable (10) | Acceptable (6–9) | Neutral (5) | Unacceptable (1–4) | Totally unacceptable (0)

It may be tempting to attribute this difference to the supposed greater importance of wine and dining in Quebec. Moreover, Quebeckers may have attached a greater value to a gift of wine, perhaps assuming it to be a fine French vintage as opposed to a bargain-bin special—and therefore presuming a greater sense of potential obligation. Then again this kind of explanation is rooted in outmoded stereotypes. Of more importance is the fact that once again where there are regional differences Quebeckers stand out as more critical. They seem to be saying that Quebec is a modern society that sets very high standards for its politicians.

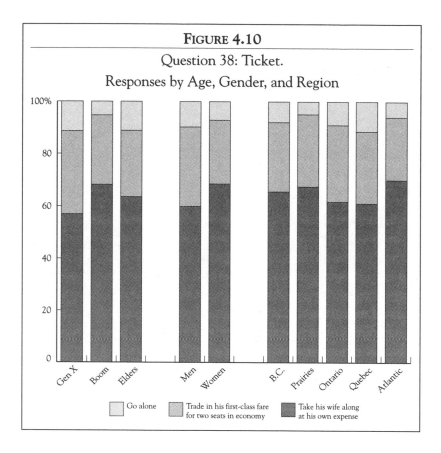

FIGURE 4.10

Question 38: Ticket.

Responses by Age, Gender, and Region

☐ Go alone   ▦ Trade in his first-class fare   ▪ Take his wife along
                     for two seats in economy   at his own expense

This message, which we have encountered already, shows up again in the next chapter.

CONCLUSION

It is difficult to ignore the brittleness of Canadians' opinions about gifts and gains. The scenarios we described are relatively minor in comparison with some of the scenarios of other types. No politician is going to get rich from occasional dinners and cab rides, whereas a secret 'arrangement' with a government contractor may be a lot more lucrative than a pension plan. Gifts

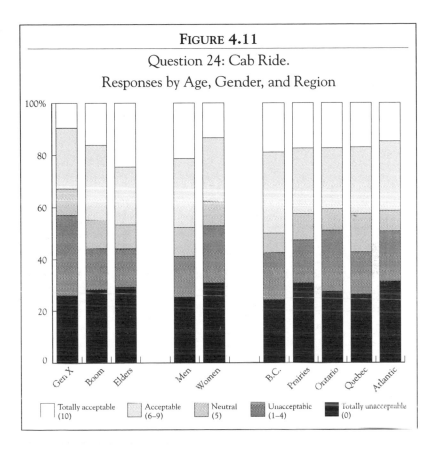

FIGURE 4.11

Question 24: Cab Ride.

Responses by Age, Gender, and Region

| | Totally acceptable (10) | Acceptable (6–9) | Neutral (5) | Unacceptable (1–4) | Totally unacceptable (0) |

and especially gains seem to be 'hot-button' issues for Canadian politicians. They are, after all, clear examples of preferential treatment for politicians solely because of their position. Even perks that are accepted in the private sector get respondents' backs up when an apparently over-privileged politician is involved.

Aside from a fairly sustained age gradient, the respondents are rather uniform in their feelings about political gifts and gains. Some mitigating factors may affect the way different subgroups view a situation, but the one strong pattern seems to be that familiarity breeds contentment, with gains at least. Those who do not have access to perks tend to be resentful of those who do, and this provides a good explanation of the respondents' overall stinginess with gains like the cab ride home.

We didn't include a question specifically on the parliamentary pension plan because presumably it would be hard to find anyone outside of Parliament who actually approved of it, especially in its previous form that allowed MPs to begin drawing a pension as soon as they left the House. We did, however, ask if people thought that politicians were 'very well paid'. An overwhelming 90 per cent agreed with this statement, and almost two-thirds agreed strongly. It seems reasonable that this belief could underlie the rejection of even small perks for public officials—if they are already overpaid, then nickel-and-diming the public for little extras here and there is all the more outrageous. We may not begrudge them every gift someone else presents to them, but we're not going to let them take anything else from 'our' public pocket.

Courtesy of Pritchard.

Chapter Five

PATRONAGE

It is hard to imagine patronage being considered a Good Thing. The word conjures up special treatment, the political trough, 'jobs for the boys', and a host of unsavoury political practices. In essence, political patronage refers to the practice of dispensing favours, often appointments or contracts, to political supporters in recognition of past political service.[1] Little wonder it is often considered a species of political corruption.[2] And yet, in some circumstances patronage is seen to be not only good, but noble. To be a patron of the arts is to be known as a generous benefactor, someone on whom orchestras, art galleries, and theatres have come to rely. How does the term 'patronage' lose its positive qualities when it moves into the political realm?

The first point to recognize is that patronage in the arts does have a dubious underside. Most patrons are content to give their support without asking for much, if anything, in return. Others are much more demanding, requiring the city, art gallery, or university to meet stringent requirements. Early patrons of the church built cathedrals in exchange for control over the lives of the congregation and the right to make appointments of minor officers.[3] Some modern patrons only wish their name to be well-displayed, but this itself can cause controversy, as when tobacco companies sponsor sporting events. These features of patronage may not be particularly repulsive—after all, who can afford to look a gift horse in the mouth these days—but even the most benign forms of patronage assume some kind of exchange.

The second point is that patronage in politics is inconsistent with the ideal of political equality. We can live with the idea that in some circumstances the privileged should be permitted to show off their wealth and status if it means a public benefit of some kind. Who will resent them for their day in the sun if the church gets a new roof or the hospital a new wing? But in the realm of politics the money being spent on appointments and contracts belongs to taxpayers, not to the politicians dispensing the largesse. Not unreasonably, taxpayers would like to see their money spent according to a public rationale and well-understood rules. The patron of the arts may use his or her discretion in selecting worthy projects, but the modern state requires a more systematic and objective set of rules. Since the public officials who set themselves up as patrons seldom provide these rules, citizens sometimes conclude that they are using public funds for their own ends. As for the people they appoint, Canadians worry that their commitment to public service is about as enduring as the amount of time it takes to line their pockets.

Patronage is inconsistent with equality in another way: the patron and the client are in a personal relationship of mutual dependence. Clients need the contacts and opportunities that patrons can provide; patrons need clients who can be counted on to provide political support at critical times. Either one can withdraw their support from the other, and there can be vigorous competition among patrons for the support of particular clients,[4] just as clients will compete with one another for the favours of their patrons. The problem is that relationships of dependence, even mutual dependence, influence political decisions. Confronted with a problem, the official who owes her job to the party boss must think not only about the most appropriate response, but also about what the boss wants or what the party expects.

Rewarding friends of the party, regardless of their abilities, is not a recipe for good public policy.

Bureaucracy, which implies government by rules, and democracy, which implies informed and independent political choice, are the enemies of patronage. Bureaucracy reduces and channels discretion, forcing politicians to defend their choices on grounds of merit rather than loyalty. Democracy challenges politicians to devise a broad electoral program in place of one based on narrow personal ties. As the appeals of bureaucracy and democracy grew in the twentieth century, patronage as a form of political organization declined.[5] But it did not disappear. In spite of being inconsistent with the requirements and implications of political equality, patronage still exists and no political party has shown much resolve in abolishing it. We will see in this chapter that although Canadians are hesitant about condemning patronage completely, they are much more comfortable with appointments based on merit. They know that the modern party requires loyalty and that on occasion loyalty must be recognized, but they also know that the modern state requires efficiency and standards of performance. If obliged to choose, they will choose the latter.

How Can Patronage Be Defended?

Even though the practice of patronage must struggle now to achieve respectability, a limited defence can be mounted. The main reason for keeping patronage around is as a means of rewarding supporters where few other rewards are available. This is not a defence of patronage, but it is the bedrock rationale. The two areas in which supporters have traditionally expected rewards are appointments and contracts. In this chapter we discuss appointments because they underline the personal quality of the patron-client relationship and because they feature so prominently in contemporary discussions of patronage.

No Defence Is Needed

It is possible to argue that so little patronage exists now that no defence of it is really needed. According to this view patronage is a vestige of another era and will, presumably, die out altogether eventually. This view has a certain superficial appeal. When the majority of government jobs were filled by party loyalists and most contracts went to traditional supporters, patronage was worth talking about. In the nineteenth century, political leaders regarded the partisan use of patronage as a constitutional principle: 'Whenever an office is vacant, it belongs to the party supporting the government,' wrote John A. Macdonald. And that view has persisted. In 1953, James Gardiner, political boss of Saskatchewan in the governments of King and St Laurent, argued, 'No one should be appointed unless he is known to be a lifelong Liberal.'[6]

But of the 120,000 or so jobs in the federal public service today, only about 3,500 are political appointments.[7] And of these, many of the prominent jobs are not awarded on the strength of political attachments alone. In fact, political loyalty was probably never the sole criterion for appointment in most cases. Even in the days of Macdonald and Laurier, it was understood that appointees must be able to do the jobs they were given and patronage must be seen to be deserved.[8] These days, competence is even more important. The heads of Crown corporations or regulatory bodies must have credentials suitable for the position they are filling, and they must be acceptable to the community in which they have to work. They must also be politically acceptable, which is not necessarily the same as having the right party connections. Finally, they must fit into the government's broader appointment strategy, which means the need to balance appointments according to gender, region, and ethnic background. The government does not simply appoint party members to high-profile public positions without considering other qualifications.[9] Being a loyal political hack is not enough.

As for contracts, there are strict rules governing who gets them and how. Some are still let without tender or to preferred vendors, but that doesn't mean that they are determined solely by patronage, and there is little evidence that those who contribute to political campaigns subsequently benefit from the government's generosity. Advertising contracts are an enduring source of patronage, perhaps because they are relatively small and can be readily split to avoid rules requiring that tenders be sought. However, no one wishes to deal with firms whose products are inferior or even dangerous. The Auditor-General reminds Canadians of contracting errors, and when these can be traced to insider deals, there is almost nowhere for politicians to hide. In short, the political downside is steep.

The relatively narrow scope for patronage does not mean it has a low profile among members of the public. As we will see when we examine the attitudes of Canadians, the view persists that patronage at high levels is routine. Very few people understand the hurdles that must be scaled to be eligible for a government contract or a political appointment. Without the facts, citizens are impressed by newspaper stories and politicians are vulnerable to the slightest hint of political pay-offs.

Patronage Builds Political Systems

It may seem outrageous, but one way of defending patronage is to argue that it helps integrate the nation by providing outsider groups with access to political spoils and thus to a piece of the pie. The idea that the public sector resembles a pie to be carved up is undoubtedly repugnant to many people, but nineteenth-century political parties did not have many other ways of consolidating their support in the electorate. What they needed were trusted workers prepared to enlist the expanding electorate by promising roads, sewers, and jobs. Appeals to religion and ethnicity could be made, but in constituencies where economic expansion was on the minds of the local elite, infrastructure and investment mattered as well.

The best examples of cases where patronage promoted integration are from the United States, where in the nineteenth and early twentieth centuries, the urban machines took an immigrant population and, with the enticement of jobs and support, drew it into the party establishment in exchange for votes. Operating at the municipal level, these machines thrived in the large American cities that served as the entry point for waves of new Americans.[10] The Canadian equivalent were the machines constructed by prominent politicians operating at the provincial and federal levels, rather than in the municipalities. All provinces had these machines, and the most proficient among them—including the Mowat and Big Blue machines in Ontario, the Gardiner machine in Saskatchewan, and the Duplessis machine in Quebec—were linked directly to politicians who held public office. They allowed parties to reach into and organize the electorate, providing generations of citizens with a political identity and a tangible reason for supporting both the party in power and the political system in general.

But how reasonable is it to think that patronage will actually help draw Canadians together or encourage anyone to think in broad, national terms? The recipients of patronage may thank the party in Ottawa (or Regina or Halifax), but they know that the jobs are theirs because of what they have done for the party at the local level. And parties whose members are stubbornly local or parochial in their concerns can hardly be regarded as instruments of national unity.[11]

Of course, not all the patronage available to parties is local. There is the Senate, after all, and the bench. Unfortunately, people appointed to these positions are often lost to the party as active members. Some Senators remain staunch party organizers or bagmen, but many do not, and even if they do, it is hard to see how their activities promote national integration, except very indirectly. As for the heads of Crown corporations such as the CBC or regulatory bodies such as the Atomic Energy Control Board, these appointments are evaluated by the public in terms of the quality of the people selected. Any suspicion that the appointments have been made to placate one or another region or ethnic group brings loud objections. When Romeo LeBlanc was named Governor-General, critics in the media condemned his appointment as a corruption of the office. A staunch federalist from New Brunswick probably looked good to the Prime Minister's Office, but those deep Liberal connections worked against him in the eyes of the media.

It is true that political parties need to reward their followers somehow, and if rewards serve to strengthen parties as national institutions and bring people into the political process who wouldn't otherwise be there, we should probably be grateful. But patronage is not a particularly effective way of appealing to party loyalists. For one thing, there is simply not enough to go around. And, as a means of creating more diversity among the holders of public office, it can backfire if others in the community are offended. Those who are on the receiving end may be eternally grateful, but those who are disappointed will be forever resentful. Whether patronage performs an integrating or a disintegrating function probably depends on which side of this fence you happen to be sitting.

Patronage Appointees Are Responsive to Political Direction

The creation of a career public service that is recruited and promoted on the basis of merit did not end the patronage system, but it certainly restricted the jobs that could be handed out by any method other than competition. The idea behind a career public service was that the government would be served by the technically able and the politically independent. Laws would be applied evenly, and requests for special treatment would be ignored. Civil servants appointed by the merit system would be able to act with independence and objectivity because they were not beholden to some politician for their job.

The problem is that politicians don't always want advisers who are independent and objective. Sometimes they want political advice, and occasionally they want their friends to be rewarded. These are not noble desires, perhaps, but politics is not for the puritanical. The people who engage in it usually enjoy the exercise of power and seek to hold onto office. They sometimes reason that it is easier to do so if they are surrounded by people who feel the same way about things as they do. After all, bureaucrats will eventually be called on to exercise discretion, whether in the application of rules or in the provision of advice. So why not have some of this discretion exercised by people who have the government's interests at heart? And who fits that description better than people who have obtained their positions through the patronage process?

This line of argument assumes, of course, that the government actually has a distinctive and coherent political program. It also assumes that career public servants can't be trusted to worry about the government's political fortunes. This latter assumption may be more important than the former: sometimes governments are simply distrustful of the advisers they inherit. When Brian Mulroney became Prime Minister in 1984, he was advised to replace deputy ministers with his own political appointments in virtually every department of the government.[12] That scheme went by the board, but Mulroney did appoint two friends—Stanley Hartt as Deputy Minister of Finance, and Frank Iacobucci as Deputy Minister of Justice, neither of whom had ever before held senior positions in the public service. Did Mulroney wish to have a pair of lapdogs in those important positions? It seems unlikely. Both appointments were praised as high-quality and, in spite of their Mulroney connections, there is no evidence that these men would have been any less responsive to the Prime Minister had they been career public servants.

Although governments make patronage appointments with an eye to ensuring that loyalty to the party will be a factor in future decisions by those people, there is no way of monitoring the results. The whole idea is to put the right people in place so that you don't have to worry about what they may or may not do. Sometimes this doesn't work. Successive presidents of the CBC have eventually turned on the governments that appointed them and criticized these governments openly for their failure to support the aims of the corporation.

This point raises the question of just how responsive we want the heads of boards, tribunals, and departments to be. Obviously we must pay homage to the principles of ministerial responsibility, by which the bureaucrat serves the elected politician. But the terms of reference of most regulatory bodies assume that politicians will not interfere with their decisions. When Michel Dupuy, the Heritage Minister in Chrétien's first government, wrote to the CRTC in the spring of 1995, his purpose was to encourage that body to consider a constituent's application for a radio licence in Montreal. But he was breaking the Prime Minister's ethical guidelines, and the Prime Minister let him know, though he eventually forgave him. Even if these boards are staffed with patronage appointments, that doesn't mean you can call them up and ask for special consideration. The fact that MPs and ministers continue to make these calls, sometimes even to judges, suggests both the appeal and the limits of this defence of patronage.

Rewarding Friends Creates Community

We normally think of patronage as a political phenomenon, but the idea of patrons and clients can be a way of organizing a whole society, not just its politics. In societies based on patron-client relations, everyone is someone's patron or someone's client. Events as routine as purchasing household appliances or as special as getting married are governed by this relationship. The result is a form of social solidarity. Who you are is determined by who your patron is and whose patron you are. This traditional kind of society is hierarchical, stable, and relatively closed. Those inside know who they are; those outside know they don't belong.

This desire for identity and solidarity has some obvious dangers, including (at the extreme) militant nationalism and profound parochialism, but the alternative is to have no political identity at all and to live without any sense of community. Of course, patronage is by no means the only way to build a sense of community, but it is a useful instrument because it solidifies and personalizes relationships of power in order to establish the boundaries and requirements of community. The successful exercise of patronage develops the sense of trust and obligation that knits people together.

According to this argument, what we find repugnant about patronage—rewarding friends with favours and positions—is just the surface of a complex arrangement in which community standards are reinforced. So the local politician who knows the community intimately is well equipped to choose a reliable contractor. That contractor will do a good job because his reputation in the community depends on it. The practice of calling for tenders and selecting the lowest bidder disrupts this form of accountability. In a patronage system, both patrons and clients have greater confidence in the value of personal relationships than in general impersonal rules. Of course this means that other people, sometimes large firms with headquarters in remote places, are treated unfairly. Community presumes a 'we' and a 'they'.

Much of the patronage that we are familiar with is driven by this desire to recognize group membership and enhance solidarity. For example, the practice, favoured in the past in the Maritimes, of replacing entire road crews after an election in which the government was defeated is not intended to get better roads. The lawyers who lose their CMHC work with a change of government are not being criticized for the quality of the services they've provided. It's simply that the road crews, the lawyers, the advertising companies, and the host of others who have benefited from discretionary appointments belong to the wrong team. They are part of another community. The same applies to the wholesale removal of the Air Canada board of directors in 1985 and their replacement by friends of Mulroney and the Progressive Conservative Party.[13] Or to Pierre Trudeau's decision to find positions for hundreds of Liberals in the dying days of his government. Neither could justify these moves on the grounds of regional representation, enhanced competence, or any other rationale except a desire to reward the friends of the party.

Very few politicians, including those who campaign on the platform of ending patronage, actually reject the system all together. Rejection of the system is too easily confused with rejection of the community of party supporters, many of whom expect tangible rewards, if not for themselves, then for other members of the team. Since their side won, it stands to reason, they argue, that their party should enjoy the profits of victory, including the right to make appointments of various kinds. When John Savage of Nova Scotia publicly denounced the elaborate patronage system his predecessors had left him, he was met with vociferous criticism from his own party. Many Nova Scotia Liberals could hardly believe that their efforts were not going to be recognized. Members of the Nova Scotia public liked the Savage plan, but they did not belong to the partisan community that Savage was supposed to be leading.

Unfortunately for the defenders of patronage, the idea that the public purse should be used to create solidarity within political parties is difficult for most Canadians to comprehend. As we will see, they understand the necessity of helping one's friends, but only when it applies to their own, private relationships.

Public relationships are different. If patrons and clients exist in the arts or in business or other parts of society, that's fine. But in the public sector, the spectacle of prominent jobs and contracts going to people because of whom they know rather than what they know is too much (even in the name of community).

CANADIANS EVALUATE PATRONAGE

Anyone who has ever been in a position to hire someone knows that there are many pressures, some of them personal. In those circumstances, most people are aware that their professional responsibilities outweigh any commitment they may feel to family or friends. But what happens if the decision makers are one step removed—that is, they can't make a hiring decision, but they can use their influence. This is the way in which many political appointments are made. Political parties want to use their patronage, but they need information about whom to give it to. Getting that information requires organization, that is, people who know people.

Outside the political realm, most Canadians have no problem with this. Asked how acceptable it is to use one's influence to get a friend a job (Q6g), over 70 per cent said it was acceptable; including 27 per cent who said it was usually acceptable; 45 per cent felt it was sometimes acceptable (Figure 5.1). The fact that someone else, perhaps a more suitable candidate, might be denied the position seems to be of minor concern. Perhaps this kind of behaviour is so common that it doesn't raise eyebrows, or maybe people simply don't see it as a serious distortion of the hiring process. Certainly people are not interested in breaking the law to help a friend. We asked if loyalty is more important than obeying the law (Q54), and only 28 per cent agreed that it is (Figure 5.1). If we outlawed the use of influence to help friends get jobs, perhaps many people would no longer find it acceptable.

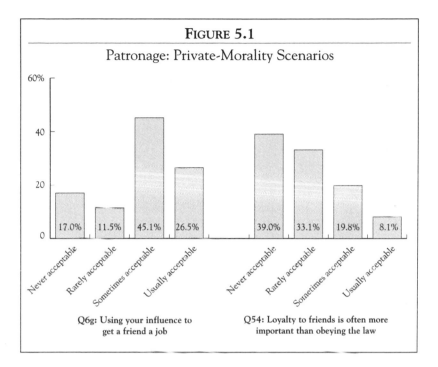

FIGURE 5.1

Patronage: Private-Morality Scenarios

17.0%	11.5%	45.1%	26.5%	39.0%	33.1%	19.8%	8.1%

Q6g: Using your influence to
get a friend a job

Q54: Loyalty to friends is often more
important than obeying the law

As we will see, however, although patronage is not illegal, it didn't get much support from our respondents. For example, if the Prime Minister were to appoint a loyal supporter to head the CBC (Q9), only 15 per cent would consider that to be acceptable, while 64 per cent said it would be unacceptable (Figure 5.2). Why would anyone object to such an appointment? Apparently, in choosing a friend of the party, people simply assume that the Prime Minister is passing over someone more competent and more deserving who should get the job. But nothing in the scenario says that another, more competent person is available, or that the person appointed is incompetent. Surely among the many party members there is someone who can lead the CBC. Probably, but being a party member is not an advantage in the minds of most people. On the contrary, it might even disqualify a distinguished candidate. But what Prime Ministers say when

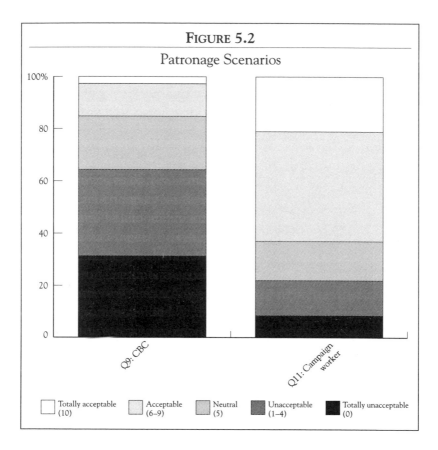

FIGURE 5.2

Patronage Scenarios

Q9: CBC

Q11: Campaign worker

☐ Totally acceptable (10)   ☐ Acceptable (6–9)   ☐ Neutral (5)   ■ Unacceptable (1–4)   ■ Totally unacceptable (0)

they appoint prominent party members is: Why should someone excellent be passed over because of an interest or involvement in politics?

The mere suggestion that loyalty to the party might be a consideration in making an appointment is enough to render it unacceptable to the majority of Canadians. So much for the idea that the government should be permitted to have its ideas reflected in the CBC's future or that the party deserves to solidify its support in the electorate. When it comes to major, high-profile appointments, no one seems to think that building or reinforcing community is much of an excuse either. Worse, in spite of their distaste for the practice, the vast majority of our sample (90 per cent) think that this kind of appointment is made 'frequently' (Q10). In short, Canadians believe that party leaders routinely reward their supporters with important, undeserved jobs.

But what happens if we make it clear that the person appointed is 'fully qualified' and the job is not specified? We asked how acceptable it is for a campaign worker to be rewarded with a government job for which he is qualified (Q11). Note that we did not stipulate that the appointee is the *most* qualified, but there is the assurance of competence. In addition, the person who gets a reward is just a campaign worker, not someone with great status in the party. And the reward is presumably consistent with this status. No ordinary campaign worker can expect to be appointed to head the CBC.

Our respondents reacted much more positively. A majority (63 per cent) find this kind of patronage acceptable, while only 22 per cent, almost three times fewer than in the case of the CBC, deem it unacceptable. Clearly this kind of patronage is judged to be at least somewhat defensible, likely because of its community-solidarity features. After all, the appointment is probably a minor one, and there is evidence that small-scale patronage is more acceptable than spectacular patronage.[14] Also, the promise of competence is crucial and perhaps more believable than in the case of the CBC. On the other hand, it is hard to see how any policy consideration should come into play in a minor appointment, so the excuse that the government needs a loyal party person to enact its program is hard to make.

The irony is that the high-profile appointment is probably more acceptable in democratic terms since it is made by an elected government with (one can only presume) a policy agenda *vis-à-vis* the CBC. The small-scale appointment is not particularly democratic, and it is certainly offensive to the idea of a neutral bureaucracy. Giving someone a government job in return for working on a campaign is a practice that has died out almost everywhere in Canada, extinguished by the need to have the law applied by a neutral public service.

To get a better feeling for the issue of neutrality, we asked whom the Minister of Justice should consider when appointing a judge. In all three of the options offered, we guaranteed competence by referring to 'qualified persons'. Option 1 allows the minister to choose among all qualified persons. Option 2 specifically allows him to 'patronize', that is, to reward a (qualified) loyal party member. Option 3 forces the minister to choose from among a short list drawn up by a non-partisan committee.

As Figure 5.3 shows, even if Canadians can get a guarantee of competence, they won't be entirely satisfied. Certainly they are not interested in giving the party the chance to reward its members if there is an alternative. Only 4 per cent of respondents chose Option 2, the patronage option. Compare that with the 34 per cent who wanted to appoint 'any qualified person'. This latter option certainly expands the pool of potential appointees and hence increases the chances of finding a superior person. That person may, in fact, be a party member. What people seem to be saying, however, is that you shouldn't begin by looking for one. It is far better to widen your search. But the majority, 62 per cent, would take it one step further. Wary that the minister may too readily find a party loyalist among the 'any qualified persons', these respondents prefer that a first screening be made by a non-partisan committee. Being qualified is not enough. Canadians want their judges appointed in a manner that ensures their independence, a position quite consistent with constitutional norms.

However, our respondents don't have much faith that politicians share their views on this point. We asked our respondents if they thought that most politicians would agree with their choice. Of those who insisted on a non-partisan screening committee, 82 per cent thought that most politicians would choose some other option. Evidently, Canadians believe that politicians will be inclined to use patronage where the public would deem

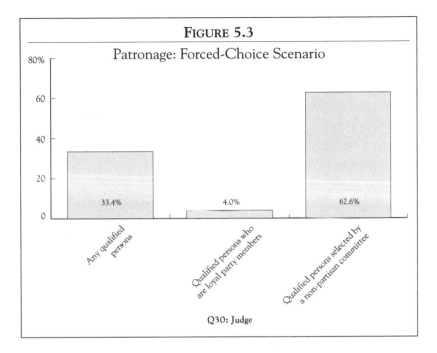

FIGURE 5.3

Patronage: Forced-Choice Scenario

Any qualified persons — 33.4%

Qualified persons who are loyal party members — 4.0%

Qualified persons selected by a non-partisan committee — 62.6%

Q30: Judge

it improper or will be unwilling to hand over their appointment authority to a non-partisan body. In either case, there is little faith that politicians will follow the instincts of Canadian citizens.

In fact, in the case of judicial appointments, the public cynicism is quite unjustified since a rather bureaucratic screening process is already well established. If people are willing to believe the worst in the absence of evidence, politicians have the task of publicizing the progress they have made in solving ethical problems. It is hard to imagine politicians not taking credit for something, especially when they have done as the public wishes.

These results constitute strong evidence that most Canadians have little tolerance for appointments that use partisan criteria. Competence is an issue, but so is the position itself. The public is willing to contemplate small-scale patronage if some level of competence can be assured, but high-profile appointments of party stalwarts are beyond the pale. Of course, as was the case in assessing gifts and gains, some respondents are more categorical than others. We turn now to the question of who is most and least critical of patronage.

WHO TOLERATES (SOME) PATRONAGE?

As we mentioned in the previous chapter, patronage is akin to gifts and gains—each is a benefit or bonus that office holders have access to through their position; what distinguishes them is who does the giving and who does the receiving. At the same time, patronage stands apart because of its long history and because it has formed the basis of organizing rather complex societies. In particular, patronage has been an important glue in Canada's history. Recently, though, that glue has been losing some of its adhesiveness. But are there groups that it still sticks to more readily than others?

Age: Is There an Old Boys' Network?

There are at least two plausible explanations of the relationship between age and views on patronage. On the one hand, it could be argued that as people get older they develop firmer views of what is ethically proper and that as a consequence their ethical standards become more and more rigid. According to this view, we should expect younger respondents to be more lenient towards patronage. On the other hand, since patronage used to be practised more extensively than it is now, older people may have seen it at work, may even have benefited from it, and may be more inclined to emphasize its merits than its limitations.

Our findings consistently support the first of these positions over the second. Recall that the majority of our respondents found it either usually or sometimes acceptable to use one's influence to

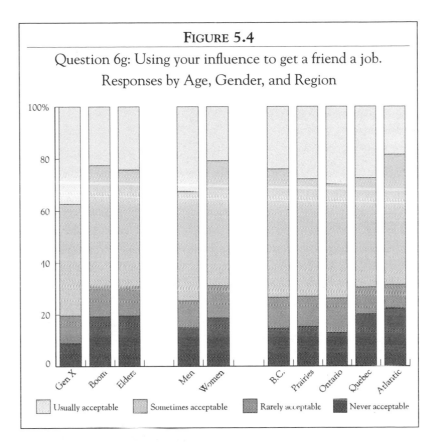

FIGURE 5.4

Question 6g: Using your influence to get a friend a job.
Responses by Age, Gender, and Region

get a friend a job. There is very little difference between Boomers and Elders on this issue, but Generation Xers are more inclined than both to support this position (Figure 5.4). Similarly, while fewer people were prepared to agree that loyalty to friends was more important than obeying the law (Q54), Generation Xers were more in agreement that the others (Figure 5.5). These differences are small in terms of the scale (about 0.3 points in each case), but they are statistically significant.

More important, the differences carry over into the realm of patronage itself. Remember that very few people liked the idea of the Prime Minister appointing a loyal supporter to head the CBC

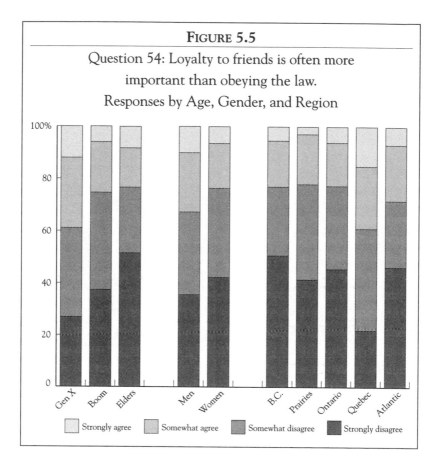

FIGURE 5.5

Question 54: Loyalty to friends is often more
important than obeying the law.
Responses by Age, Gender, and Region

(Q9). The overall average was about 3 on the 10-point scale,
where the higher you go, the more acceptable the act. Generation Xers are half a point above the mean; Boomers and Elders
are both below it (Figures 5.6 and 5.7). Although there is very
little difference between the latter groups, Generation Xers are
statistically different from both, meaning that they are more tolerant than those in the older age groups.

The same findings apply in the case of the party worker rewarded with a government job (Q11). Everyone is more tolerant
of this scenario than of the CBC appointment (the average score

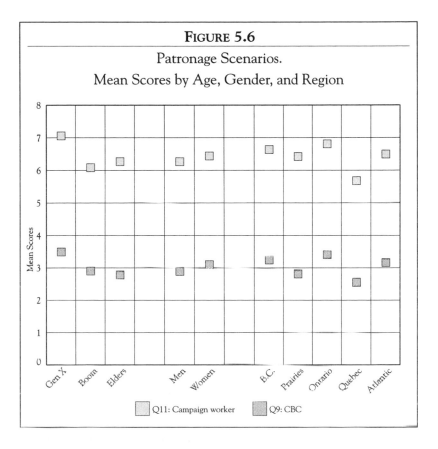

FIGURE 5.6

Patronage Scenarios.

Mean Scores by Age, Gender, and Region

is over 6 on the 10 point scale), but Generation Xers score over 7 on the scale, a full point above Boomers (Figure 5.8). Once again, members of Generation X look more kindly on patronage than anyone else. The same applies to the appointment of judges. Very few respondents thought it a good idea to select from the qualified party faithful, but Generation Xers were almost twice as likely to take this position than others (Figure 5.9). Though their attitudes are in the vicinity of the rest of the sample, they are consistently found on the more tolerant end of the scale. Our data thus support the hypothesis that they are generally more permissive. Older Canadians may indeed have had

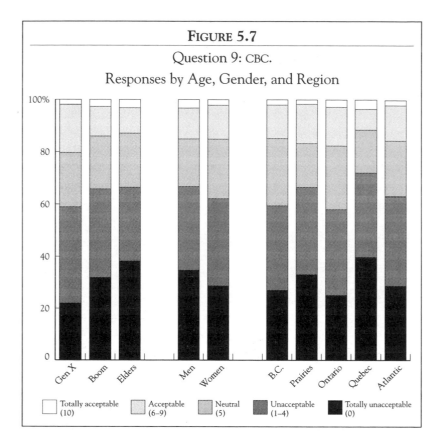

FIGURE 5.7

Question 9: CBC.

Responses by Age, Gender, and Region

Legend:
- Totally acceptable (10)
- Acceptable (6–9)
- Neutral (5)
- Unacceptable (1–4)
- Totally unacceptable (0)

Categories: Gen X, Boom, Elders, Men, Women, B.C., Prairies, Ontario, Quebec, Atlantic

more experience with patronage, but rather than strengthening their support for it, as we suggested, this seems to have solidified their disfavour. If they are more aware of the supposed benefits of patronage, they may be even more aware of its drawbacks.

Gender: Is There an Old *Boys'* Network?

The answer to this question is yes and no. Yes, on the questions involving personal morality. Men are more lenient than women. Women are more inclined to say that it is never or rarely

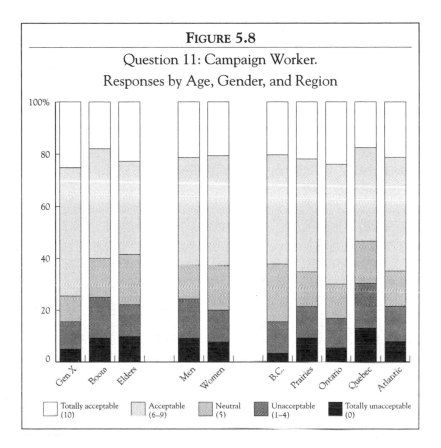

FIGURE 5.8

Question 11: Campaign Worker.

Responses by Age, Gender, and Region

acceptable to use influence to help a friend get a job. About one-third of the men thought this was usually acceptable; only 21 per cent of the women agreed. On the question of whether loyalty to friends is more important than obeying the law, about two-thirds of men disagreed, compared to three-quarters of women. In both cases these differences are statistically significant.

It is difficult to know the reason for these differences, but women's discomfort with the idea of backroom networking may simply be due to their experiences. The 'old boys' network' is just what it says it is: women are not included. On the other hand, women may simply have different, less tolerant, views about the

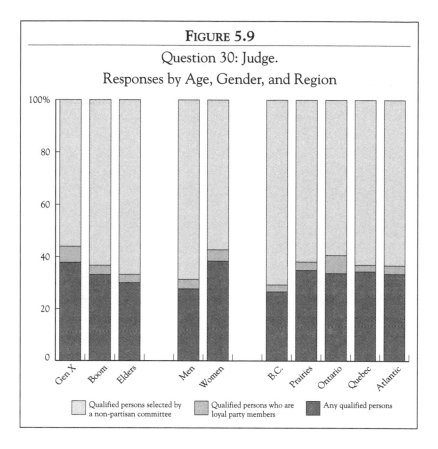

FIGURE 5.9

Question 30: Judge.

Responses by Age, Gender, and Region

Qualified persons selected by a non-partisan committee | Qualified persons who are loyal party members | Any qualified persons

propriety of using any criterion other than merit to make appointments. According to this interpretation, women employ a different ethical standard, a perspective we discussed briefly in Chapter 2.

There is no way of knowing which of these positions is correct, but it is interesting to note that once we move to the realm of patronage itself, the differences between men and women evaporate. Whether we are considering the appointment of the head of the CBC or a campaign worker who gets a government job, men and women give essentially the same responses. On the matter of the appointment of the judge, women are more inclined to prefer 'any qualified candidate', whereas men like the committee screening. But when it comes to the option of appointing a qualified party member, men and women are virtually identical in rejecting this position.

If men and women reason differently about patronage, there is little evidence of it in these results. Women are not as comfortable as men with using their influence in a private situation, but when it comes to evaluating politicians' behaviour they endorse the same positions as men. As we have said before, these results do not mean that men and women arrive at their conclusions in the same way, only that the conclusions themselves are essentially the same.

Regional: *Where* On the Old Boys Network?

There is some reason to believe that tolerance for patronage will vary from one region to another. The idea of regional political cultures, discussed in Chapter 1, may not apply to every aspect of political ethics, but it does seem to apply to patronage. Duff Spafford, for instance, found that highway employment markedly increased at election time in Quebec and New Brunswick and to a lesser extent in Nova Scotia.[15] This suggests that patronage is part of the political culture in the east and perhaps particularly so in Quebec. Spafford points out, however, that this phenomenon could be observed only before 1965; there does not seem to have been any similar tendency toward highway hiring after 1966. Of course, what politicians do and what the public thinks they should do are two different things. The fact that patronage is practised more extensively in some parts of the country than others doesn't mean that people in those regions necessarily approve of it.

On the matter of using one's influence to get someone a job (Q6g), region matters in a rather minor way. People in Quebec and Nova Scotia are slightly more inclined to say this is never acceptable (21 per cent compared to 14 per cent in the rest of the country), but beyond that there are hardly any regional differences. Far more impressive is the matter of loyalty versus obeying the law (Q54). Here respondents from Quebec constitute a distinctive minority. Whereas between 42 per cent in the Prairie provinces and 52 per cent in British Columbia strongly disagree with the view that loyalty to a friend is more important than obeying the law, only 22 per cent of Quebeckers disagree. Looked at the other way, almost 40 per cent of Quebeckers agree with this statement, while the comparable figure in Ontario is 23 per cent, in British Columbia 23 per cent, in the Prairie provinces 22 per cent, and in the Atlantic provinces 30 per cent. Whether this tells us that Quebeckers consider friendship to be very important and the law to be man-made and fallible is a matter of speculation. Once again, however, we get a feel for the possibilities by examining the data on patronage itself.

If many Quebeckers feel somewhat ambivalent about the law when it conflicts with loyalty to one's friends, there is no culture of permissiveness, at least not political permissiveness, underlying these responses. On the contrary, when it comes to political patronage, Quebeckers are consistently the least tolerant of our respondents. On the matter of the CBC appointment, the average response on the 10-point scale (where lower scores mean less tolerance) was 3.0. Quebec's average was 2.5, the lowest among the regions and significantly lower than the most tolerant respondents, those living in neighbouring Ontario, where the average score was 3.4.

These differences show up yet again on the question of the campaign worker who gets a government job. While people in all regions were much more willing to forgive this piece of political generosity, once again Quebeckers were the least tolerant. The mean score of 5.7 for Quebec is well below the mean of 6.4 for the whole sample and markedly different from all others except those who live in the Prairie provinces. It is only on the matter of what to consider when appointing a new judge that Quebeckers are no different in their responses from anyone else.

In the matter of political patronage, the most important regional difference is between Quebec and the rest of Canada. Differences among the other provinces are minor and never statistically significant. It is Quebec that is different, and Quebeckers emerge as the least tolerant of patronage. This will come as a surprise to many, given the long-standing tradition of patronage in that province. However Canadians in general have been regularly reminded that Quebec in the 1990s is not the society of the pre-Quiet Revolution period, when many stereotypes appear to have been formed. As Bourgault and Dion note, 'Quebec's originality lies in its history of striking contrasts. Nowhere else has a government moved so quickly—in barely twenty years—from one extreme to the other, from systematic patronage and widespread conflicts of interest to a rigorous regime of controls over official behaviour.'[16] Our data show not only that the government has moved, but that public attitudes have moved as well.

CONCLUSION

It is not easy to defend patronage in modern-day Canada. The virtues of the practice are often exaggerated, and the vices are all too obvious. Whatever may be said for patronage as a means of integrating the country, creating a sense of community, or providing political direction, there is no reason to believe that patronage is the only way to accomplish these goals. Though politicians have not denied themselves the opportunity to reward their friends, they have restricted themselves to some degree, partly at least because they recognize that the public expects them to use other means to achieve their ends.

Our research shows clearly that Canadians have little patience with high-profile patronage appointments. The appointment of judges and the holders of other high offices ought to be based on other criteria, almost certainly merit and competence. And if party loyalists happen to be chosen, they had better possess large amounts of those qualities because the party hack is presumed to be unable to carry out the tasks of office. Canadians clearly value competence and they doubt that loyalty to party is the best way of obtaining it.

As we move across generations and across the regions of the country, attitudes do differ somewhat. These differences remind us that the world of politics, and political ethics, is not one of unbroken consensus. Pockets of opinion exist, and these include those who are inclined to be more forgiving of patronage (Generation Xers, for example) and those who are inclined to be less forgiving (the residents of Quebec, for instance). But these differences should not obscure the overwhelming view that patronage is not the preferred means of selecting public officials in Canada. Whatever people may think about their private choices, and many of them are quite prepared to help their friends when the opportunity arises, they don't want politicians doing the same.

Roy Peterson, *Vancouver Sun*.

Chapter Six

✠

LYING

✟

We all know we are not supposed to lie. Our mothers told us, our fathers reminded us, and schoolteachers reinforced the message. They knew the dog didn't eat our homework or that our baby brother didn't throw up all over it. They knew the truth: we didn't get it done. And yet we keep on lying or at least trying to.

It's probably because lying is so easy. Relative to the other commandments—thou shall not steal, thou shall not kill, and so on—it is possible to lie without much organization, or even much thought. And besides, it's usually much easier to justify than murder. You hate that tie your boss is wearing, but he seems to like it. So what are you going to say, when he asks you about it? 'I hate that tie?' Maybe, but you will at least think it over.

Some of you will tell a bold, outright untruth: 'Wow, you look fabulous in that tie!' Others will pretend not to hear, will mumble something, or will find some way of suggesting the equivalent of 'no comment'. Or you might get really inventive and suggest that it is not as nice as some of the other ties he has worn. Either way, unless you have a particular point to make about fashion, you will think twice about the unvarnished truth.

If you decide on something short of the truth, it won't be difficult to justify. There are after all other values at stake. You don't want to hurt people's feelings over something so trivial. So, let's call this a little white lie, one that you are telling to protect other people. What makes it a little white lie is the context. True, you may be breaking a commandment, but you have weighed the consequences and made a pragmatic decision.

When politicians lie, they will tell you the same thing, that is, that the consequences of telling the truth are simply worse than lying. The problem with this excuse is that no politician wants you to get the impression that they are lying all the time. It gets you thinking about other times and other situations when you've wondered if what you were hearing was the truth. If lies are actually necessary, and we're not saying they are, it would be helpful if there were some rules that limited the kinds of lies that can be told.

Do such rules exist? Are there certain circumstances in which telling the truth is absolutely required, and others in which some fudging is acceptable? In this chapter we find out just what kinds of lies Canadians are prepared to tolerate. And we find out whether some Canadians are more tolerant than others.

How Can Lying be Defended?

In this chapter we use the term 'lying' in a broad fashion to include all forms of deception. Obviously, straightforward mistruths are part of this definition, but so are failures to tell the whole truth, evasion, breaking a promise, and withholding information. These are all linked by the common quality of deception, which 'involves intentionally causing (or attempting to cause) someone to believe something which you know (or should know) to be false'.[1]

We deliberately begin with an inclusive definition and a very high standard. The truth, the whole truth, and nothing but the truth—anything short of this is lying. Put this way, telling the truth may not look all that attractive. If there are no exceptions, and weaselling or fudging is not allowed, how many will sign up for total honesty?

Most of us are prepared to consider at least some situations in which lying, if not acceptable, is at least understandable and rather tempting. Politicians think the same way. Let's consider some of the more popular excuses that politicians employ for engaging in deception. First, the scope and scale of the lie, second, whether the lie was intentional, third, the matter of extenuating circumstances, and finally, the question of lying to protect personal privacy.

Scope and Scale

Suppose the lie is just a small one, a little white one. Suppose that the politician who tells it has never lied before. How much should we make of this? In May 1989, Lyall Hansen, Minister of Labour in the British Columbia government of Bill Vander Zalm, admitted that he had not corrected a lie told by one of his officials. The official, Bert Hick, had publicly denied that he had been pressured by a prominent supporter to conduct a public referendum on the advisability of building a pub in a residential area. Rather than create the impression that he might be subject to political influence, Hick chose to lie about it when asked by reporters. Hansen, the minister, didn't tell the lie, but he didn't help anyone discover the truth either. When it all came out in the media, Hansen's only defence was that the whole issue was of no real importance.

Now it must be admitted that at one level this isn't a big issue. This is about building or not building a pub. Hick, the bureaucrat, lied to avoid embarrassment. Hansen presumably wanted to avoid embarrassment as well, or he would have immediately corrected Hick's story.

Naturally, the Opposition wanted Hansen to resign. Opposition critic Moe Sihota argued that, 'The public has a standard of expectation from those in public life and that expectation is that you be honest and you be truthful.'[2] Is Sihota right, or, put another way, are politicians like Lyall Hansen permitted no deviations whatsoever?

It is almost certain that any member of the public would have preferred the truth on this occasion to the piece of loose deception that satisfied Hansen. The real question is, what happens next? If the truth-telling standard is absolute, then politicians get only one chance. It doesn't matter if the lie is big or small; it doesn't matter if it was an outright lie or a lie of omission; and it doesn't matter if this is the first and only time. Of course, with this kind of standard we may go through politicians in a hurry. And if we don't, it will only be because these sorts of deceptions go on unrecorded and unrecognized.

But they can't be excused either. Lying to avoid embarrassment suggests a weakness of character. It is not the scope of the lie that matters—this may be very limited— it is what the lie says about the qualities of the politician. Citizens justifiably doubt not only the politicians who tell lies, but also those whom they associate with, and the institutions in which they work. So while the lie itself may be trivial, its consequences are not, not for politicians and not for political institutions. Here is a case in which public figures are not the same as private individuals, because their lies always have public repercussions. In many respects, there is no such thing as a little white lie in politics.

Extenuating Circumstances

Perhaps the most common defence of lying on the part of politicians is that they did it in defence of the public interest. Considered this way, lying is actually a noble thing to do. While the political leader risks the criticism of her followers, she is compromising herself for their benefit. Or at least she thinks she is.

Lying in the public interest is most frequently associated with foreign-policy crises in which telling the truth to citizens will put the nation at a disadvantage, since the truth would then be available to the country's enemies. This line of defence assumes that lying to one's enemies is a good idea, and there are many who question that tactic. And even if it is a good idea, most politicians would prefer to avoid the issue or make some vague, ambiguous pronouncement, than to tell an utter false-hood. That is why many foreign-policy deceptions have an element of truth in them. When Lyndon Johnson asked Congress to support the Vietnam war because American ships had just been attacked in the Gulf of Tonkin, the actual attack had occurred a few days earlier. President Johnson concocted a fic-tional battle in an inventive parallel of the truth.

Not all public-interest arguments for lying involve foreign policy. In 1970 Pierre Trudeau invoked the *War Measures Act*, claiming that the country was in a state of 'apprehended insur-rection'. Was it? The RCMP could produce no evidence, and there is at least some reason to think that the *War Measures Act* was a way of convincing Canadians that the *indépendantiste* movement in Quebec was led by a core of radical, violent revolutionaries who had to be crushed. Once again, there is some truth to this analysis, but many Canadians were persuaded that Prime Minis-ter Trudeau had confused the national interest with his own political agenda.

Another time that lying is proposed as the safer option is when the truth could cause trouble. We all enjoy free speech, but your right to speak your mind does not extend, in the classic example, to yelling 'fire' in a crowded theatre. In fact, even if there is a fire, a more responsible way of behaving would be to leave the building in a quiet and orderly manner. Might it not be acceptable for politicians to lie if the alternative is public unrest and chaos? During the devastating ice storm in January 1998, there was a risk that Montreal would lose not only power, but also water service. The authorities decided not to inform the public of this risk in order to forestall widespread panic. Once the lights were back on and the crisis was over, the public was not particularly upset by this failure to tell the whole truth. Then again, the water never did stop flowing: how this decision would have been judged if the water had been cut off without warning is something we can never know. If the authorities had been completely forthright, the stranded residents could at least have prepared for a water shortage.

And that is one of the problems with lying in the public interest: no one knows for sure if the public interest is actually served when officials do not reveal information on which the public might wish to base a decision. In a democracy we take great pains to avoid letting a governing party, let alone a single politician, define the 'public interest'. Whatever that elusive phrase actually means, the very expression suggests that the public is involved. Lying 'implies contempt for the intelligence and courage of the public. It implies the public official knows better than the average citizen what is in the public interest; worse, it implies that the public cannot be trusted with the truth.'³

Unintentional Fibs

The definition of lying used above implies that it is an intentional act. But if someone stops you on the street and asks for directions to St James' Anglican Church, and you inadvertently send them to St James' Presbyterian, you didn't really lie to them; you simply made a mistake. The problem is that while you may know your own intentions, others don't. The person you misdirected will conclude either that you made a reasonable mistake (they may even blame themselves if they are Canadian) or that you deliberately misled them.

The problem with intent as a criterion for anything is that it can never be measured directly and always has to be inferred. The psychology profession, though still divided over many things, agrees with this maxim: you can never know someone's intentions. All you have to go on is their behaviour. They may assure you that they didn't intend to mislead you, but there is no way you can know this for a fact.

This hard truth has not stopped us from making difficult decisions in criminal law based on assessments of the accused's intentions. If the truck driver meant to run over the cyclist, it's murder; if he was careless or negligent, it is manslaughter. In politics we have to do the same thing, that is, make informed judgements about intentions, but often with much less information than a judge or jury might have. We listen to the story, often filtered by the media and attacked by the Opposition, then make a judgement about its plausibility.

In the summer of 1996, Glen Clark, who had recently become Premier of British Columbia, was accused of lying about the dismissal of John Laxton, former chair of B.C. Hydro. Laxton had been involved in an insider-trading scandal on a hydro project and Clark had fired him and several of his colleagues. Or at least that's what Clark thought. When it was revealed that Laxton had continued to work for a B.C. Hydro spin-off company, the opposition Liberal Party accused Clark of lying. Whether or not Clark intentionally misled the province depends on whether he knew about Laxton's new job.

Politicians hate to be caught in a lie, but they don't especially like having to admit that they misled anyone either, even unintentionally. If Clark was unaware of Laxton's new employment, then he didn't lie about firing him, but he also didn't have a grip on the facts. This is why politicians expect complete honesty from their advisers. It may be tempting for politicians to remain in the dark so that they can maximize 'deniability', but this tactic almost always backfires. Politicians who try to avoid lying by not learning the truth inevitably appear (at best) either ignorant or not in control.

One way to avoid uttering an unintentional falsehood is to keep quiet. In spite of their public image, not all politicians are loudmouths in search of a microphone or a TV camera. And when microphones and cameras are unavoidable, in election campaigns for instance, politicians soon learn to avoid predicting the future unless they enjoy the benefits of time travel. When Jean Drapeau, as mayor of Montreal, claimed that the upcoming 1976 Olympics could no more lose money than a man could become pregnant, cartoonists enjoyed the opportunity to dress him in maternity clothes, a lesson lost on none of his contemporaries.

But keeping quiet has become increasingly difficult as politicians try to respond to demands that they make their political intentions clear. When the Opposition Liberals were preparing for the 1993 election, they did so by creating the Red Book, a compendium of promises to which they evidently expected to be held accountable. It sounds like good democratic practice, but what happens when you decide that some of these promises aren't worth keeping? The honourable thing to do would be to say so and accept the criticism that you made a mistake.

That is what the Liberals tried to do about the GST. In the course of announcing that his budget would not repeal the GST in spite of his party's promises to the contrary, Paul Martin, the Finance Minister, said, 'We made a mistake. It was an honest mistake.' Was it? That depends on whether you think the Liberals ever actually intended to repeal the tax, and on this issue there is room for doubt.[4] The party had no alternative in hand when it made the promise, and it never developed one in the two years before Martin's admission.

Promises that aren't kept are not lies unless those who made them had no intention of keeping them.[5] Since no government will freely admit to mendacity on that level, it comes down to plausibility. In the case of Sheila Copps, who pledged to resign her seat if the GST was not scrapped, there is reason to believe that she thought the promise was made in good faith. Who knows about the other members of her party or their other promises?

The 'Pinocchio Syndrome'

The problem with all these defences for lying is that they have such fluid boundaries. If lying is justifiable in certain cases, who decides which cases allow lies? Who prevents the situations in which lies are justifiable from expanding to cover all of public discourse? In March 1997 a brouhaha erupted in Quebec over the publication of André Pratte's *Le Syndrome de Pinocchio*,[6] in which the author asserted that lying has become ubiquitous in politics and that politicians no longer have any compunction in failing to tell the truth. In his view, the various excuses for lying have drained it of all moral content. Lying has become just another tactic, to be used when it results in more success than the alternative. Just as politicians choose between raising or lowering taxes, between paving a road or building a school, between signing or not signing a treaty, they choose between lying and telling the truth purely through objective consideration of what will bring them more approval.

Predictably, politicians in Quebec did not take this thesis well. Nor did they appreciate a call-in television program that accompanied the publication of the book, which asked the public to 'vote' for the politicians who lied the most.[7] The next day, the National Assembly unanimously (with the lone exception of ADQ leader Mario Dumont) passed a motion denouncing the purpose, tone, and content of the program. The motion's sponsor, the then leader of the Quebec Liberal Party, Daniel Johnson, denounced the program and the book as attacks on the intellectual integrity of members, candidates, and the whole political system.

Politicians everywhere hate being called liars. In most democratic legislatures, members are specifically forbidden to accuse each other of lying. In fact, just the week before the Pinocchio fracas exploded, Johnson himself had been admonished by the Speaker of the Assembly for calling Premier Lucien Bouchard a liar during a debate. Pratte would argue that this sensitivity is a clear example of 'the truth hurts'. And, moreover, that this sort of righteous indignation isn't fooling anyone. He suggests that politicians' lies are motivated by the same desire to please (or not to displease) others that is behind our own little white lies.[8] We don't want to offend our boss over an ugly tie; politicians don't want to lose votes over an ugly policy. But Pratte and others don't accept this application of private-realm logic to the public sphere. His argument is that any political lie cheapens and demeans the system, that it is the use of lies as elements of policy—not accusatory books or TV programs—that offends the honour of the system.

THE PROBLEM OF PRIVACY

There is one further dimension to lying in public life that complicates the issue. We have examined various defences of political lying and various rebuttals to them, but we have concentrated on lies about public matters. Is a politician's private life a genuine public matter as well, about which a lie is of public consequence? Do politicians even retain what we would recognize as a private life? Is it ever justifiable to say 'no comment'?

If you think about your own life, the answer will come to you quickly, and the answer will be yes. People don't generally stop you on the street and ask about your sex life, but if someone did it is unlikely that you will feel compelled by any moral imperative to tell them the truth, the whole truth, and nothing but the truth. This is simply a personal matter, not a public one, and so the only problem in this scenario is with the question, not the answer.

How much changes when a person is elected to public office? It seems unreasonable to argue that a politician gives up all rights to privacy, but it is equally unreasonable to suggest that those who elect politicians should know nothing about their personal lives. The answer seems to be that you can refuse to tell the truth, or only tell part of the truth, if the matter at hand has no bearing on public policy. The criterion here is that of relevance. If a politician's personal life is not relevant, there is no harm, in fact there may be some good, in declining to tell all.

The problem, of course, is to establish what is relevant. There are some who would argue that every part of a politician's private life—the type of car she drives, the number of children she has, her religion, whether or not she smokes and so on—is relevant to everything that she does. Most of us are used to categorizing people by this type of information, and some will use it to make sweeping character judgements. But if they do, politicians won't really have private lives at all.

If you take the more restricted view that a politician's personal life is important only if it has a direct bearing on what that politician must decide, then circumstances will play a large role in your judgement. If the Minister of Finance is a smoker, is this something Canadians should know? It sounds like a personal matter, until you think about taxes on cigarettes. What about the Minister of Health: if he declined to reveal whether he smokes, should we insist that he owes us the truth, given his portfolio?

It's not easy to decide because here we have two competing values, privacy and openness. And more often than not it is politicians who choose between them, not because they have a better sense of what is relevant, but because they alone are in possession of the personal information. If the Prime Minister smoked pot in his youth, he may be inclined to dodge questions about this simply because he doesn't think it's relevant to the job he is doing. He makes the call. Mind you, declining to answer questions like that takes courage. For one thing, a failure to answer directly will be taken by many as a sign of guilt. Second, if the Prime Minister did not smoke pot, he will be strongly tempted to tell the truth even though the question may constitute an invasion of his privacy.

When reporter Pamela Wallin asked the then Opposition Leader, John Turner, in 1988 if he had a drinking problem, he denied the rumour. The press was divided over whether the question should have ever been asked. Some argued that it was an unforgivable breach of privacy, although no one went as far as to suggest that if he did have a drinking problem, Turner would have been justified in lying about it.

If Canadians are inclined to be cautious about probing into the personal lives of politicians—and we will see that they are—it is likely because personal questions are sometimes hard to answer truthfully, with the result that the answers are often next to useless. When journalists persist in trying to root out the details, they are the ones who are likely to find themselves being criticized while politicians are excused, to some degree, for not sharing the truth with the world.

CANADIANS EVALUATE PRIVATE LYING

An epidemic of cynicism, combined with a resurgence of interest in so-called traditional values, has led many to consider lying as not just a political tactic but an indicator of character (or the lack thereof). For them the context of the lie no longer matters because they no longer care what may have prompted a lie, and they feel free to see any falsehood as evidence of a serious character flaw.

At the same time there has been an unprecedented interest in, and knowledge of, what once were the private lives of public officials. The voters, frustrated by public declarations they don't believe, have turned a magnifying glass onto the personal behaviour of politicians, looking for clues to help distinguish the truly abominable candidates from the merely unpalatable. And sometimes this magnifying glass lands directly on the lies politicians tell in their own personal lives—what we will call 'private lying'. When this happens, how likely is it that the public will assess the personal conduct of politicians fairly?

Privacy and Honesty

In exchange for enhanced knowledge and power over others, office seekers give up a measure of control over part of their lives. They are transformed by election from private citizens to public figures. This is a choice freely made, and those who make it can hardly expect to enjoy the privileges of office without sacrificing their personal affairs to constant scrutiny.[9]

And yet surely there must be limits. The public has a right to know, but does it have the right to know everything?[10] According to former NDP leader Ed Broadbent, 'Canadians have no business knowing about the private lives of politicians unless there is a problem—such as excessive drinking—that may affect their ability to govern. . . . Anything that does have a direct impact on public policy the public does have a right to know.'[11] According to this standard, Pamela Wallin's question was actually not out of line, but many other routinely asked ones are.

It is difficult to find a balance between public interest and the right to privacy, and no two people will agree on how much of a politician's private life should become part of the public domain. This tension is intensified by the public's search for honesty, as any attempt to stop even an intimately personal line of questioning implies a cover-up. The principle of privacy requires that some things remain off limits; the principle of honesty demands forthright and unwavering candour. At a certain point these principles inevitably clash.

Our study indicates that the public is aware of, but hasn't yet decided how to resolve this clash. In the abstract the public is ambivalent about politicians' right to privacy (Figure 6.1). They overwhelmingly (87 per cent) agree that politicians should expect less privacy than ordinary citizens (Q43), and most (59 per cent) believe that the personal conduct of cabinet ministers is relevant to their leadership abilities (Q50). They are only moderately insistent that MPs should have higher ethical standards

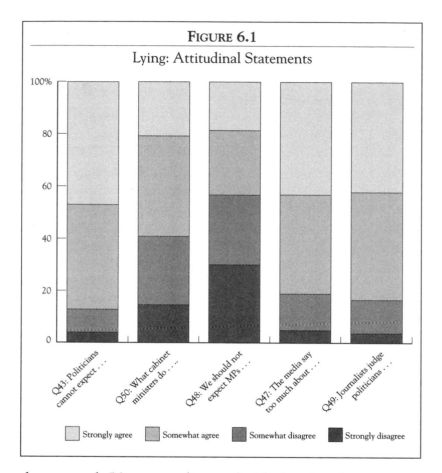

FIGURE 6.1

Lying: Attitudinal Statements

Q43: Politicians cannot expect . . .
Q50: What cabinet ministers do . . . .
Q48: We should not expect MPs . . .
Q47: The media say too much about . . .
Q49: Journalists judge politicians . . .

Strongly agree   Somewhat agree   Somewhat disagree   Strongly disagree

than normal: 56 per cent disagreed with the view that MPs must have higher standards than those they represent (Q48).

But while private lives may be fair game, Canadians also feel strongly that the media do not play fair when they investigate personal matters. Over 80 per cent of respondents believe that journalists report too much about the private lives of politicians (Q47), and the same percentage think that journalists judge politicians by standards they themselves could not meet (Q49). There appears to be a suspicion of hypocrisy on the part of the media.

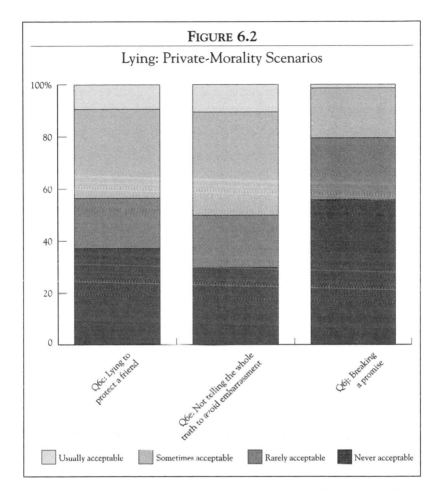

FIGURE 6.2

Lying: Private-Morality Scenarios

Q6c: Lying to protect a friend

Q6e: Not telling the whole truth to avoid embarrassment

Q6j: Breaking a promise

Usually acceptable   Sometimes acceptable   Rarely acceptable   Never acceptable

It seems that the public wants personal information about politicians but is unhappy with the style and tactics of the primary source of this information. Since private citizens cannot usually obtain this information themselves, they must rely on news media that they think goes too far. This distaste for the behaviour of media may show itself as sympathy for politicians when their private lives become media fodder.

In Chapter 2 we saw that the respondents were strongly attracted to honesty in general as an important value. Fifty-eight per cent chose honesty as the most important value over equality, compassion, freedom, and tolerance (see Figure 2.1). What happens to this principle under actual conditions? Thirty-seven per cent of respondents said that lying to protect a friend (Q6c) is never acceptable, and another 19 per cent said it is only rarely acceptable (Figure 6.2). The question about not telling the whole truth to avoid embarrassment (Q6e) splits the respondents more evenly—half find this sometimes or usually acceptable. The strongest condemnation is for breaking a promise (Q6j): almost 80 per cent of the respondents believe that it is never (56 per cent) or rarely (24 per cent) acceptable. They seem to recognize that certain situations may warrant less than complete honesty, but support for the principle remains strong even when it competes against the demands of friendship or self-image. Breaking a promise in particular seems to evoke a strong negative reaction.

In general Canadians believe strongly that honesty is the best policy but as with any policy, that there are cases in which flexibility is warranted. There are routine situations in private life that might excuse a lie, but lies must be the exception, not the rule, and above all promises made must be kept. What we now ask is whether those willing to accept some dishonesty in personal situations will grant the same latitude to public officials faced with similar dilemmas.

Politicians' Private Lies

The efforts of politicians to manage their personal affairs are always complicated by the public's interest in what their representatives do behind closed doors. Two of our scenarios concerned lies told by politicians about their private lives. The responses to the first of these, about the cabinet minister who keeps his visits to a psychiatrist from the Prime Minister (Q7), reveal no consensus. The wide variety of responses may indicate that the public is not entirely sure how such a situation should be

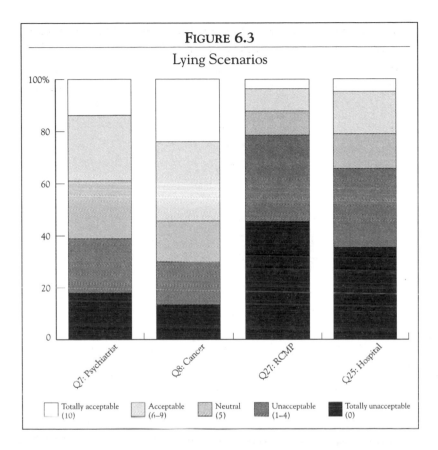

FIGURE 6.3

Lying Scenarios

Legend:
- Totally acceptable (10)
- Acceptable (6–9)
- Neutral (5)
- Unacceptable (1–4)
- Totally unacceptable (0)

handled, and the relative tolerance for this scenario may suggest that lies told by one politician to another are judged less harshly than those told to the public (Figure 6.3).

On the other hand, the public is generally tolerant of the scenario in which an MP who has cancer denies the fact when questioned by a journalist (Q8). Almost one-quarter of respondents found this totally acceptable, and half scored it a 7 or above. The public, which otherwise so highly values honesty, is willing in this case to accept an unequivocal falsehood.

There are two plausible explanations here. As the popularity of 'disease-of-the-week' TV movies indicates, there is a lot of sympathy immediately accrued to anyone stricken with what may be a fatal disease. In a society obsessed with health and longevity, there are few matters more personal than one's medical condition. Even the divisive issue of Quebec separatism did not prevent the outpouring of public support, from across the country for Lucien Bouchard when he lost his leg and nearly his life to necrotizing fasciitis—the 'flesh-eating disease'.

The role of the media is important in this question. The many respondents who thought the media were too eager to report the intimate details of politicians' lives (Q47), may also be reacting not so much to the fact that the politician denies his condition, but to the involvement of a journalist in the question, and the apparent unwarranted invasion of privacy the question represents. Recall Pamela Wallin's questioning of John Turner.

It would seem that despite the overwhelming choice of honesty as their most important value, Canadians are willing to excuse lying in certain, especially personal, circumstances. Not surprisingly, those who selected honesty first from the list of values scored even these private lying scenarios as less acceptable than did other respondents. This consistency extends as well to questions of personal morality. The public appears to evaluate the private lies of public officials in much the same way as they evaluate lying in their own lives. Respondents who said that not telling the whole truth to avoid embarrassment (Q6e) was never acceptable were much more likely to deem the related behaviour in both Q7 and Q8 equally unacceptable. This strong relationship holds similarly between all parts of the private-morality scale and these two scenarios.[12] Claims of an unfair 'double standard' find little support here.

One other scenario (Q28) that examined private lying presented a politician who is asked by a journalist whether he is seeing a marriage counsellor. The respondents had to say how they thought the politician should reply (Figure 6.4). Only 21 per cent chose the unvarnished truth ('Yes, I'm seeing a counsellor').

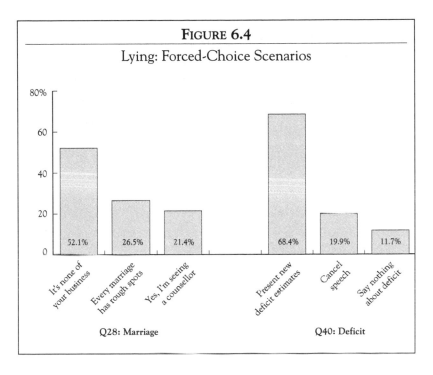

FIGURE 6.4

Lying: Forced-Choice Scenarios

Q28: Marriage
- It's none of your business: 52.1%
- Every marriage has rough spots: 26.5%
- Yes, I'm seeing a counsellor: 21.4%

Q40: Deficit
- Present new deficit estimates: 68.4%
- Cancel speech: 19.9%
- Say nothing about deficit: 11.7%

The respondents' previous insistence on honesty and on the limitations on a politician's privacy is not borne out here. Apparently it's not essential to tell the whole truth to nosy reporters. In fact, more than half the respondents (52 per cent) preferred that the politician invoke an explicit right to privacy ('It's none of your business'), and the rest (26 per cent) approved of his evading the question entirely ('Every marriage has its rough spots').

In the abstract, politicians' fear that their private sphere is constantly shrinking would seem to be justified. In practice, however, the public is much more forgiving of lies told in the defence of privacy. The issue of private lies brings out the tension between the public's low opinion of politicians and its low opinion of journalists: there appears to be a line which, when crossed by the latter in their pursuit of reportable tidbits, causes the public's sympathy to shift to the former.

CANADIANS EVALUATE PUBLIC LYING

Because politicians are public officials, there is a sense in which any lies they tell are 'public' lies. The distinction we are making here is between lies politicians tell that pertain to their private lives and those they tell in the context of governing. The former has been referred to as 'private lying'; we will refer to the latter as 'public lying'. In the case of public lying, a further distinction should be made between lies that are told in the course of performing the duties of a particular public office and lies that take the form of broken promises. Unkept promises are sometimes called passive lies to underline the fact that no action actually takes place. Politicians who fail to keep their promises may, initially at least, have had no intention to mislead. Active lies, falsehoods told in the conduct of public office, are deliberate deceptions.

Active Public Lying

When politicians lie in the course of their public duties, their defence is almost always couched in terms of extenuating circumstances, usually something like, 'If I told the truth, terrible things would happen.' As we indicated earlier, there are many examples of this kind of lying in the realm of foreign affairs, where heads of states and foreign ministers deliberately misinform both their adversaries and their own citizens, apparently for the sake of some greater good. Lying to your enemies is often justified as a form of statecraft, but lying to citizens normally requires a more elaborate rationalization.[13]

In the scenarios presented to our respondents, it was clear that there were negative consequences to telling the truth. The degree of these negative consequences differs. Q27 concerned a cabinet minister who lied to Parliament in order to protect the reputation of his deputy minister. Even though revealing knowledge of this investigation would damage the reputation of someone who might not be guilty and possibly compromise the investigation itself, most respondents condemned this lie (Figure 6.3). Almost 45 per cent of those surveyed found the minister's lie totally unacceptable, and 78 per cent ranked it as unacceptable. Only 10 per cent found it acceptable. As these data indicate, there is remarkably little deviation from the view that lying in Parliament is reprehensible.

It may not be necessary to lie directly to engage in active public lying. According to Paul Ekman, 'there are two major forms of lying: concealment, leaving out true information; and falsification, or presenting false information as if it were true.'[14] Whereas in Q27 the minister falsified by misleading Parliament, in Q40 the minister is given the possibility of concealment. The Minister of Finance is scheduled to give a speech on the economy when he learns that the deficit is much larger than expected. The majority of respondents, two-thirds, advised that the minister should present the new deficit estimates (Figure 6.4). Approximately 20 per cent suggested that the minister should cancel the speech; only 11 per cent suggested concealment: 'Make the speech, and say nothing about the deficit.'

How consistently does the endorsement of honesty as a guiding value flow through to the conduct of public affairs? We saw earlier that the consistency between honesty and private matters was relatively high. It is even higher in the realm of public lying. In the case of the minister's lie in Parliament, members of the public who find it never or rarely acceptable to lie to protect a friend are much more inclined than those who find it sometimes or usually acceptable to judge the minister's actions as totally unacceptable.[15]

When we move to the case of the Finance Minister, our respondents who find it never or rarely acceptable to avoid embarrassment by not telling the truth are slightly more inclined to insist that the minister present the new budget estimate. There is consistency here, but it is not very strong. The strongest message from this question is simply that it is better to tell the truth than evade the issue. Citizens, it seems, prefer to get the facts even if they are unpleasant.

Passive Public Lying

In the case of passive lying, the public figure may have every intention of keeping a promise but for some reason is unable to do so. Recall that when asked how acceptable they found 'breaking a promise', 56 per cent of respondents said it was never acceptable, and only about 20 per cent found it either sometimes or usually acceptable. Let us see how that attitude translates into the political realm.

In Q25 a political party promises not to close any hospitals but discovers later that it must break this promise (Figure 6.3). Even though it is only one hospital, and even though there may be good reason for the decision, 35 per cent of the respondents found the action totally unacceptable and two-thirds found it unacceptable to some degree.

These findings reflect a growing impatience with broken election promises among those, namely citizens, who live with the consequences. In the GST case, outlined earlier, the deputy Prime Minister, Sheila Copps, had campaigned in 1993 on a promise to resign her seat if her government failed to repeal the tax. She eventually did so, but only when public opinion polls indicated that her attempts to renege (she explained that she had only been 'shooting from the lip' when she made the vow) were disastrously received.

The increasing propensity of politicians to make election promises in the form of contractual obligations has almost certainly contributed to the public's exceptional intolerance on this matter. This device—which was seized upon by the authors of the Liberal Red Book, the Ontario Conservatives' Common Sense Revolution, and, in the United States, Newt Gingrich's 'Contract with America'—is obviously designed to capitalize on precisely this frustration with broken campaign promises. But not surprisingly, none of these 'contractors' has managed to keep their covenants sacred, thus deepening the holes they originally dug.

It is conceivable that politicians and the public simply see promises in different ways. For members of the public, there is not much difference between breaking a promise in one's private life and breaking an election promise. Those who find it never acceptable to break a promise in their personal lives are much more inclined to condemn politicians who break promises than are those who find it sometimes or usually acceptable to break promises.

It seems likely that, for politicians, election promises constitute an open, constantly negotiable platform that may or may not be implemented, depending upon how basic assumptions and governmental options evolve. For the public, promises are promises, pure and simple: they should never be uttered without the resolve to keep them.

POLITICAL LIES: WHO IS THE MOST TOLERANT?

In previous chapters, some patterns of variation in responses have emerged. The Canadian public is in general not pleased by many of the activities we described, but some groups are less pleased than others. Do the same patterns that characterized conflict of interest, gifts and gains, and patronage hold true for lying? Should we again expect older women in Quebec to embody the strictest standards and harshest criticism of political behaviour?

Age: Is the Generation Gap a Credibility Gap?

In the case of age, earlier work has suggested that older respondents are likely to be less tolerant of ethical lapses than younger

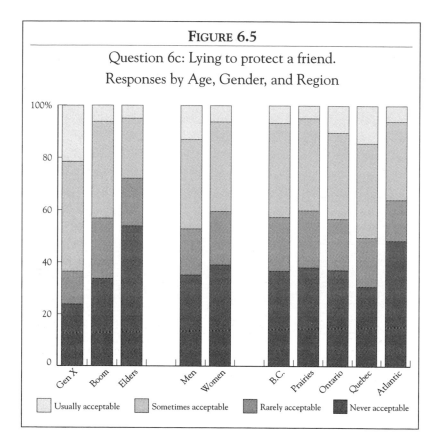

FIGURE 6.5

Question 6c: Lying to protect a friend.
Responses by Age, Gender, and Region

☐ Usually acceptable   ☐ Sometimes acceptable   ▨ Rarely acceptable   ■ Never acceptable

ones. It may be that the older one gets, the less patient one becomes with public officials who don't tell the truth. Or it is possible that people born at particular times share particular political experiences that shape their way of looking at things. People who lived through the Watergate period may remember that expressions like 'stonewalling' and 'non-denial denial' were adapted to apply to a particularly Nixonian brand of lying.

Our research shows that age is very important in explaining attitudes toward lying. It is clear that the older our respondents, the less likely they are to tolerate either lying to protect a friend (Figure 6.5) or lying to avoid embarrassment (Figure 6.6). For

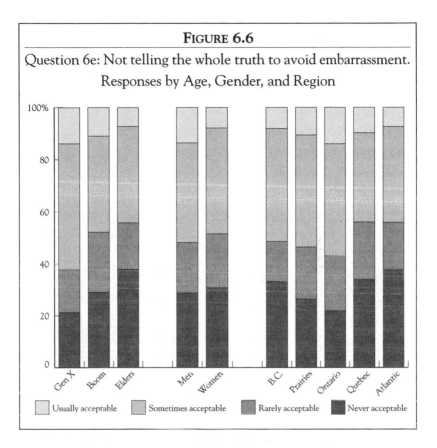

FIGURE 6.6

Question 6e: Not telling the whole truth to avoid embarrassment.
Responses by Age, Gender, and Region

Usually acceptable   Sometimes acceptable   Rarely acceptable   Never acceptable

example, the proportion of Elders who said that lying to protect a friend is 'never acceptable' greatly exceeded those who said that it was 'usually acceptable' by 54 to 5 per cent. Among Generation Xers the tendency was quite different: only 24 per cent chose 'never', while 22 per cent said 'usually'. These findings underscore once more a substantial age gap in attitudes about personal morality.

This gap closes somewhat when it comes to breaking a promise: older people are still significantly less inclined to find this acceptable, but the main message is that a majority of all respondents (55 per cent) think it is never acceptable to break a

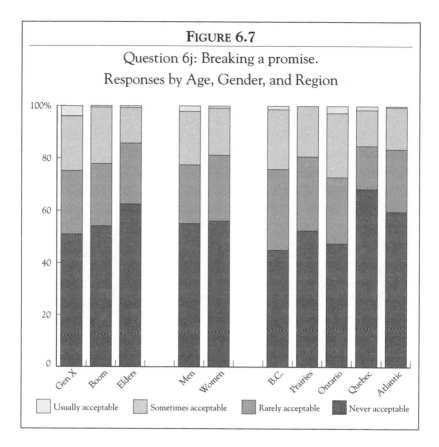

FIGURE 6.7

Question 6j: Breaking a promise.

Responses by Age, Gender, and Region

☐ Usually acceptable ☐ Sometimes acceptable ■ Rarely acceptable ■ Never acceptable

promise (Figure 6.7). Compare that with 37 per cent who say it is never acceptable to lie to protect a friend, and only 29 per cent who say the same thing about lying to avoid embarrassment.

Does age have a similar effect on tolerance for political lying? Yes and no. In the case of the private lying—the cases of the visit to a psychiatrist (Q7) and the MP with cancer (Q8)—age matters in precisely the way it matters above: the older the respondents, the less likely they are to approve of either of these scenarios (Figure 6.8). Take the psychiatrist example. Only 7 per cent of Generation Xers thought it was totally unacceptable for the MP to lie about seeing a psychiatrist, but 30 per cent of Elders felt

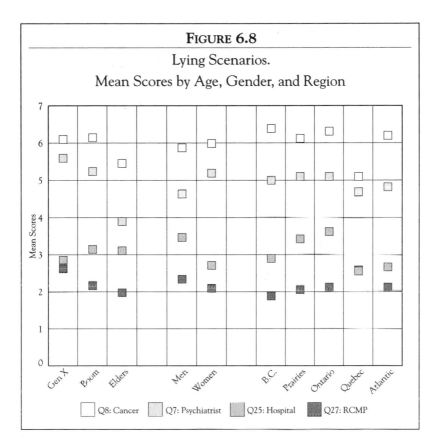

FIGURE 6.8

Lying Scenarios.

Mean Scores by Age, Gender, and Region

this way (Figure 6.9). The same pattern is seen in the case of the MP with cancer (Figure 6.10). When it comes to the marriage counsellor, however, there is no age pattern among those who would say, 'Yes, I'm seeing a counsellor' (Figure 6.11). There is, however, a significantly greater likelihood that older respondents will decline to answer, whereas younger people are more likely to evade the question by saying that all marriages have 'rough spots'.

Age is important in private lying; but what about public lying? Here the pattern is not so clear. Once again, older people are less tolerant of the minister who lies in Parliament to protect

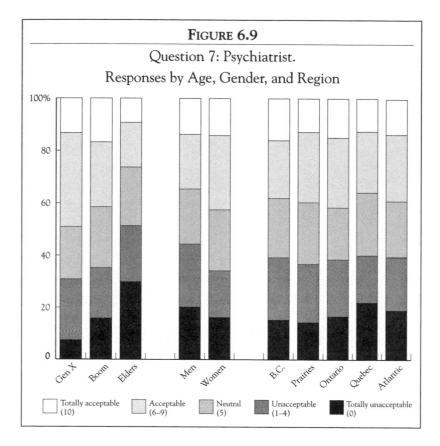

FIGURE 6.9

Question 7: Psychiatrist.

Responses by Age, Gender, and Region

Totally acceptable (10) · Acceptable (6–9) · Neutral (5) · Unacceptable (1–4) · Totally unacceptable (0)

his deputy, but only one in five respondents found this act acceptable to any degree (Figure 6.12). The more intriguing responses involve the Finance Minister who has to make a speech and the hospital promise. In the former case, older respondents are more inclined to make the speech and say nothing about the new budget estimates (Figure 6.13). This is a bit surprising, given their preference for the unvarnished truth in other situations, but remember that older people are also less inclined to volunteer information in private matters.

The hospital promise is revealing in that here age is of no consequence whatsoever (Figure 6.14). Large proportions of all

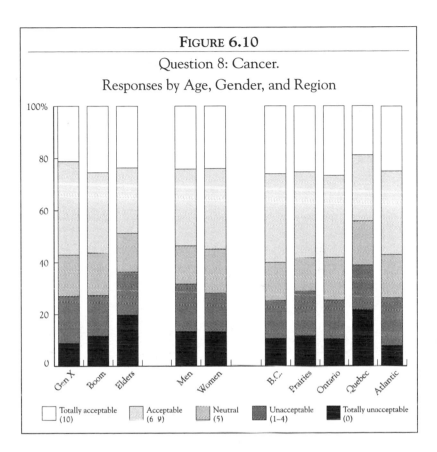

FIGURE 6.10

Question 8: Cancer.

Responses by Age, Gender, and Region

| | Totally acceptable (10) | | Acceptable (6 9) | | Neutral (5) | | Unacceptable (1–4) | | Totally unacceptable (0) |

generations find breaking a promise 'unacceptable', and smaller proportions, once again from all age groups, find it 'acceptable'. In short, age matters most for private lying and less for public lying.

Gender: Lies— A (Wo)man's Prerogative?

What about gender? In the case of private lying, we actually find the reverse of the usual trend: women are more inclined than men to forgive the cabinet minister who fails to report his visit

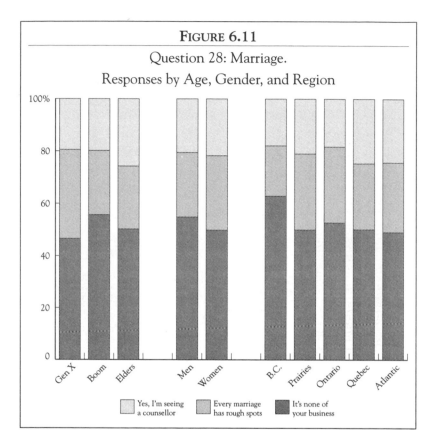

FIGURE 6.11

Question 28: Marriage.

Responses by Age, Gender, and Region

☐ Yes, I'm seeing
a counsellor   ☐ Every marriage
has rough spots   ■ It's none of
your business

to the psychiatrist. This pattern does not hold, however, for the MP with cancer and the MP who is asked about his marital problems. In these other private lying cases, men and women respond in much the same way. Is there something about the psychiatrist situation that explains the difference? We noted the general willingness of Canadians to limit a journalist's right to pry; perhaps women are even more protective of privacy when it is another politician being kept in the dark. Or, since the psychiatrist episode is a passive private lie, whereas the others are active, it may be that women are more willing to accept a 'don't ask, don't tell' rule of thumb for private lies.

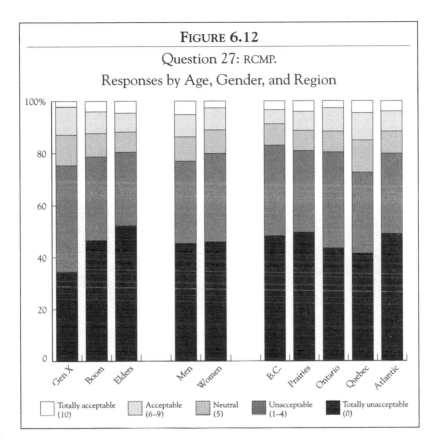

FIGURE 6.12

Question 27: RCMP.

Responses by Age, Gender, and Region

Age tends to be more relevant in private lying. Gender really matters more in circumstances of public lying. There is virtually no difference between men and women on the question of lying in Parliament to protect a deputy (Q27). But on the matter of election promises—the hospital question (Q26)—women are far more inclined to find the breaking of that promise unacceptable. They are also much less likely to suggest that the Finance Minister give the speech and say nothing about the new budget estimates. In public matters, women are more likely to demand the complete truth; in personal matters they are slightly more willing to keep the whole truth private.

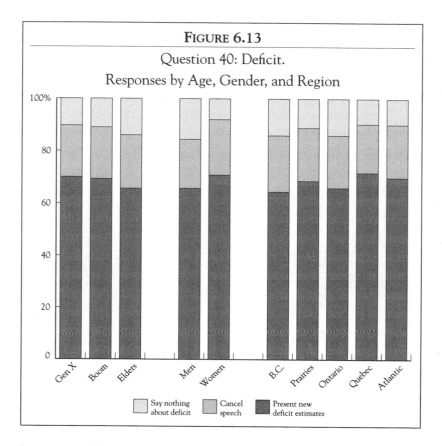

FIGURE 6.13

Question 40: Deficit.

Responses by Age, Gender, and Region

Legend:
- Say nothing about deficit
- Cancel speech
- Present new deficit estimates

Region: Lies From Coast to Coast?

Finally, does the willingness of Canadians to tolerate lying depend on where they live? In their personal lives, residents of the Atlantic provinces are significantly more inclined to think that lying to protect a friend is 'never acceptable'. As for lying to avoid embarrassment, Atlantic residents are joined by Quebeckers and British Columbians as the least tolerant. For example, well over 30 per cent of respondents from those provinces think that lying to avoid embarrassment is 'never acceptable', compared to only 21 per cent of Ontarians and 27 per cent of those living on the Prairies. A similar pattern applies to promise breaking: this time

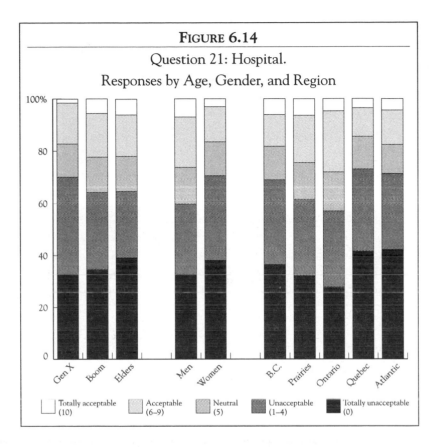

FIGURE 6.14

Question 21: Hospital.

Responses by Age, Gender, and Region

| | Totally acceptable (10) | Acceptable (6–9) | Neutral (5) | Unacceptable (1–4) | Totally unacceptable (0) |

Quebeckers are the least tolerant (68 per cent said it was 'never acceptable'), and Ontarians and British Columbians are the more accepting. Again, the conventional wisdom about Quebec seems to be reversed.

It is somewhat surprising that this pattern doesn't hold up once we move to the evaluation of politicians. In the realm of private lying, there are no regional differences whatsoever with respect to the minister who lies about the psychiatrist (Q7) or the MP queried about his marriage problems. As for the MP who lies about having cancer, Quebeckers are clearly outliers: they are significantly more inclined to find this response unacceptable.

A possible explanation is the resonance this scenario has with the real-life case of the late Quebec Premier Robert Bourassa, who concealed his own cancer through a successful re-election campaign.

When it comes to public lying, the only area in which region matters appears to be that of passive lying. In the matter of the hospital promise (Q25), Atlantic respondents and Quebeckers are once again by far the least tolerant. Over 42 per cent of Atlantic respondents and roughly the same proportion of Quebeckers found the failure to keep the hospital promise 'totally unacceptable', whereas only 28 per cent of Ontarians, 32 per cent of Prairie residents, and 37 per cent of British Columbians felt the same way. It is tempting to ascribe the difference to the frequency of grandiose and spectacularly broken election promises that have plagued the Atlantic economy, and perhaps one particularly resonant but ambiguous promise—the separation issue—in Quebec. Of course, every region has its own favourite broken promise, and nowhere were the respondents close to forgiving such breaches of faith. These results suggest that there is a regional effect in the matter of lying, but it does not apply evenly to every scenario. And while residents of Atlantic Canada and Quebec tend to be less tolerant, this holds only for certain issues.

CONCLUSIONS

When it comes to questions of political ethics, lying is a familiar yet complex issue. Citizens who are mystified by the ins and outs of patronage and conflict of interest still have clear opinions about lying and what constitutes an excusable lie. And despite suggestions that the public's analysis of 'levels of truth' in politics is erratic and rudimentary, Canadians appear to apply relatively consistent standards in evaluating lies in both private and political life.

With respect to the excuses we previewed, the scope and scale of the lie doesn't seem to matter much. In the case of the hospital closing, it was only one hospital, but the response was still very negative. As for extenuating circumstances, the overall preference was to tell the complete truth, although significant minorities of respondents were prepared to cancel speeches rather than face the music, and the 'no comment' option was a clear preference in one case. Of course, the last case involved a private matter, and by and large, privacy issues provided the most acceptable excuses for lying. Though the public eagerly consumes trivia and tidbits about political lives, there is a large reservoir of forgiveness available to politicians who spin, evade, or divert the attempts of journalists to probe their personal secrets. No one wants their dirty linen washed in public; it would seem that citizens are willing to extend this sentiment to individuals whose public statements they may not trust. In fact, they may actually applaud a politician who shows the courage to counter an impertinent question with a clear, unapologetic 'none of your business'.

Politicians should not, however, hope to exploit this sympathy by misleading anyone about public matters. The waters of understanding do not run that deep. Dishonesty about substantive issues always results in particularly toxic political fallout. What the study shows is that voters really do insist on being told the truth, whatever the consequences.

Politicians face a difficult challenge as they attempt to encapsulate and aggregate the hopes, desires, and public funds of complex modern democracies. When they lie to those who have put them in power, they challenge a crucial foundation of the governing process. Theoretically, the people place their trust in politicians, even though in practice many people do not trust individual politicians. Politicians who hope to improve their image should worry less about what the public thinks about them as persons, and more about what they think of them as representatives and holders of the public trust.

Conclusion

✦

CANADIANS
SPEAK OUT

✦

Now that we've listened to the opinions, comments, suggestions, observations, and rants of our sample of Canadians, what have we learned? Can we figure out any way to get closer to that 'good government' our country's founders described? Or is ordering up a new one the only way we'll get some peace? We know Canadians are not especially pleased with their public officials. Whether that anger is a blind rage or a frustrated but rational concern is something that we need to understand. Our results suggest that it's some of each. The media are fond of portraying the public as harbouring a deep, unreasoning hatred for politics. But there is a good deal of consistency and coherence in the way the public evaluates the conduct of elected officials. What drives the approval ratings downward is just the failure of politicians to realize that certain behaviour—no matter how legal, traditional, or commonplace amongst their colleagues—is out of bounds. They also misinterpret and ignore the areas in which the public mood is relatively generous and try to overcompensate.

THE GREY ZONE OF POLITICAL ETHICS

There is no doubt that politicians and the public alike are able to recognize what constitutes blatantly corrupt behaviour. In some developing countries, such practices as bribery are ingrained and unavoidable, having essentially become part of the system. Although bribery is not entirely unknown in Canada, it is clearly considered extraordinary. It can't survive without secrecy and cover-ups, because the public disapproves of it so intensely. We actually asked our respondents to evaluate an instance of bribery: 93 per cent said that 'giving money to a police officer to avoid a speeding ticket' (Q6h) was never acceptable. We didn't ask about bribery in the public realm because ample studies have shown that the tolerance is equally low.[1]

Because bribery is illegal, it is tempting to equate illegality with this kind of hard-core, clearly corrupt type of activity, and to assume that what the law proscribes is a nucleus of what the public condemns. Unfortunately, most ethical dilemmas in public life are not so simple, since the public appears somewhat willing to countenance some types of patently illegal behaviour. More than a quarter of our sample said it was sometimes or usually acceptable not to declare purchases to customs (Q6i), and more than half thought the same about paying cash to a plumber to avoid taxes (Q6b, see Figure 7.1). It is easy to come up with explanations for these attitudes: the tax burden in Canada is not light, the amount of money involved is not large, the chance of getting caught is remote, and 'everyone does it'. So the temptation is strong, and people feel justified in cheating at the margins. Why should the government take so much of our money, especially when it doesn't do such a great job of spending it efficiently? If they can save a little here and there, who does it hurt? As people grow more cynical about the political system, they feel less inclined to support it and blindly turn over their pay cheques.

The law is not a perfect encapsulation of morality, for there are some illegal acts that most people condone. In fact, the realm of political ethics encompasses a much larger number of technically legal actions that many people would nevertheless not accept as proper. Like the 'grey market' in products that are not

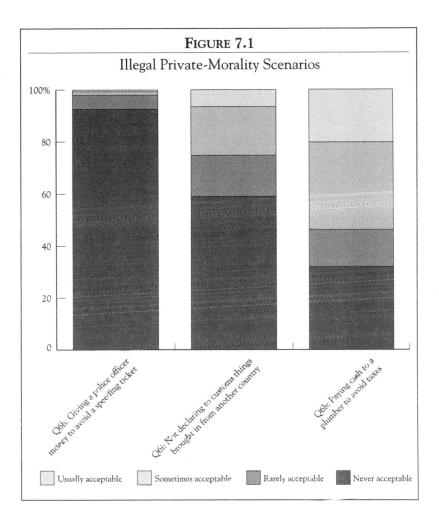

FIGURE 7.1

Illegal Private-Morality Scenarios

approved for sale but are not technically illegal, this is a 'grey zone' of unrestricted but ethically dubious activity. The fundamental problem here is that much of what politicians do is unavoidably located in this grey zone. They are sailing without a chart in treacherous waters where shoals and reefs of strong but untapped public opinion lie beneath the surface, and there are almost certain to be frequent shipwrecks.

EVALUATING TYPES OF BEHAVIOUR

We have tried to map out and investigate four different regions of this extensive grey zone. Where are the darker and lighter shades? Where are the safe passages, if any, and where should we put up giant Do Not Enter signs? More technically, what activities are acceptable and what factors and circumstances affect how the public views the actions of its elected representatives?

With regard to lying, the most important factor is the context of the lie. Politicians will find their reputations surprisingly resilient to lies and evasions that have to do strictly with their private life, but lying about public affairs is a very dangerous game. And putting a public lie in the shape of a formal promise is one of the surest ways to offend the public. To a certain extent the notion of election promises has become something of a joke, but Canadians still want to be able to believe in them.[2] They want to be able to trust what their potential leaders promise and to be able to make real choices and reasonably expect these choices to be reflected in government policy. The Pinocchio Syndrome affair showed that politicians hate being called liars just as much as the public hates lying politicians. There is common ground between these two positions: lies do not belong in politics. The trick is making this ideal into reality. As André Pratte suggested, lying will remain an efficient and effective, and therefore irresistible, tactic for politicians to use until the costs are made to exceed the benefits.[3]

Politicians are fond of defending unpopular decisions by claiming that they 'have a mandate to govern'. But the public doesn't see it that way. The winning party doesn't get the opportunity to do as it pleases for four or five years. The public backed its platform, and that is the platform that ought to be put in place. If there is a plank that may not be desirable or feasible, we ought to know in advance that it could turn out to be optional. This tells us that the idea of the Red Book or the Common Sense

Revolution is a good one. Documented and detailed campaign promises give the public a scorecard, but it is a risky strategy because it highlights every failure to achieve and turns misguided intentions into outright lies. A contract with the voters can't just be an election strategy; it has to be a governing strategy.

Pierre Trudeau asserted that 'the state has no place in the bedrooms of the nation.' Our findings suggest that the public feels it has no place in the bedrooms of the government. We may find what politicians do behind closed doors to be interesting and titillating, but Canadians don't assert some right to know about the details of clearly personal aspects of our politicians' lives. As long as it doesn't affect their ability to govern, what they do in their spare time is their own business. The good news for politicians is that the public will in fact allow them to have private lives.

Perhaps even better news is that the public resents the media's attempts to pry. When reporters are more interested in private lives than public issues, they need to be reined in. The media tend to use the public's inquisitiveness to justify their microscopic focus on private affairs—but our data suggest that this is just a convenient rationalization. If anything, the public finds personal intrusion tiresome, and might favour—as long as it is a truly private matter—a blunt, candid 'mind your own business' as a refreshing change. This is really the flip side of the honesty policy—tell the truth about what matters to all, but don't be afraid to draw your boundaries.

There is an interesting parallel between the two types of lying we discussed—public and private—and the gifts-versus-gains situation. Just as the respondents were more tolerant of private lies, so were gifts, which are private benefits, judged less harshly. Canadians may be willing to offer their politicians an unexpected amount of slack in matters confined to their private lives, but they will pull the leash taut as soon as any issue spills over into the public realm or involves the public purse. Here we seem to see the classic stereotype of the fat-cat politician enjoying the good life on the backs of the poor taxpayer.

Like other stereotypes this one contains an element of truth, but it has also been exaggerated. To be sure, many gains available to politicians are not available to others, but not all of these are free; many of them offset responsibilities and requirements that are unique to political life. The public needs to be less critical and learn more about the realities of public office, but until they do so there will be no appreciative audience for politicians who complain about their hard life or ask for a pay raise. Currently even trivial gains, like the free cab ride, just reinforce the stereotype. Politicians need to remember this and be careful. Even if a new gain is reasonable and justifiable, the public is unlikely to see it that way.

A similar message is being sent about patronage. Again, we have a stubbornly persistent stereotype of rampant patronage, which is not entirely borne out by the facts. Politicians don't help improve things when they do choose to indulge themselves. What's most clear in this type of behaviour is something of a double standard on the part of the public. While most seem willing to let friendship and connections influence their own private transactions, they object to politicians' doing the same in the conduct of public business. This is certainly not an indefensible reaction. When you get your buddy a job, you know they're competent enough, but who knows about the Prime Minister's friends? What is often forgotten is that the Prime Minister knows them and knows that he will be responsible for their performance. Loyalty doesn't preclude merit. The crucial consideration is appearance.

Appearances are also critical in assessing conflict of interest. With the other three types of behaviour it was easier to reach definite conclusions. With conflicts of interest the shades of grey are more muted and subtle. Conflict is not rejected outright as even small gains are. Rather the circumstances and mitigating factors of a particular conflict become essential to evaluating it.

The public's responses to the various conflicts we described were extremely varied. This is not necessarily a sign of inconsistency; rather it attests to the complexity of the concept. The possibility of conflict of interest is inherent in almost all political activity. It is also at the source of some of the most severe abuses of political power and the public interest.

It is no simple task to devise hard and fast rules for adjudicating different types of conflicts. That is why for so long policy makers resisted even trying to define conflict of interest. Our findings demonstrate that in this area the public is also not entirely sure where the boundaries ought to be. What is needed is a well-constructed framework that gives the politicians the guidance they want and the public the benchmarks it needs. Situational ethics are an indication of a stunted ethical sense. The public knows pretty well what it wants in the other three types of behaviour; it's not so sure about conflict of interest. So it is in this area, perhaps, that politicians have the greatest opportunity to exercise leadership. But continuing to avoid the problem won't make it go away. By confronting it themselves politicians can help the public to come to grips with and express its latent beliefs about conflict of interest.

What this adds up to is a call for a formal code of conduct, focused on, but not necessarily restricted to, conflict of interest. The sad thing is that this call has been ignored for more than two decades. Until now it has always been a question of political will. Politicians have been wary of the pitfalls of regulating themselves unless there is some benefit in increased public confidence. Though we offer no guarantee, our findings do suggest that there is one. A resolution to even part of the conflict of interest issue could help strengthen the bond between politicians and the public, and between the public and institutions of government. Apparently the public is in favour of making the contract between government and governed more explicit, as in books of election promises.

Do Canadians Speak Out with One Voice?

In summarizing our interpretations so far, we have listened to one overall public voice. But in many cases we found that there is really a multiplicity of voices—most singing the same tune in relative harmony—but distinct from one another all the same. As expected, the voice of Quebec was regularly distinguishable from that of the other regions. On the other hand, it was distinct in the opposite way from what other studies would lead us to expect. In almost every case where there was a significant difference, Quebeckers were more critical of the activities we depicted, not less. The pattern is thus not one of Quebec versus the 'Rest of Canada', but rather one of selective intensification. Canadians are all somewhat intolerant of patronage and political gains; Quebeckers are especially so. No one likes broken promises; Quebeckers dislike them especially. In Quebec, the issues are starker, and the distrust more passionate. At times this *fortissimo* refrain is joined by the Atlantic provinces, which might have been expected to be more forgiving of political misconduct, but which proved to be just the reverse.

These two regions—Quebec even more so than the Atlantic provinces—are the ones that have undergone the most extensive socio-political upheaval in the past several decades. Despite the lingering stereotypes of these regions, they have evolved from freewheeling, machine-controlled political cultures to much more responsible and meritocratic systems. The more critical attitudes in those regions may be due to progressive zeal and a reaction to the deficiencies of the bad old days. The experience with breaches of political propriety has heightened, not diminished, their disapproval of those practices.

We again had preconceptions about the differences we would find between men and women. In this case, they were largely borne out: women are less tolerant than men. The exception was in certain types of private lies, where women were more tolerant of the need to protect one's personal life in a hierarchical context of party structure. This fits the overall hypothesis that women do really think differently, or at least act differently, from men. However, if personal relationships are more important for women, as is often asserted, why do they not display more tolerance of patronage? It is also important to note that not every scenario elicited gender differences: there are broad areas—political patronage for example, or some types of conflict of interest— where men and women substantially agree.

The most apparent and persistent divisions among the respondents are in fact those between the generations. Again, the stereotypes like the persnickety senior and the permissive youth turn out to have significant basis in reality. We found that, for the most part, even where the gender and regional differences evaporated, the generation gap remained, with Generation X especially distinct from the Elders. At times the Boomers tended towards the more tolerant (or less judgemental) position of the Generation Xers; more often they were closer to the more crit-ical Elders. It may be that the Boomers are a less cohesive group, as far as attitudes toward political ethics go, than the other two. They are certainly more wishy-washy.

But here it is important to underscore an earlier caution: it is difficult to determine whether age-related factors reflect a life-cycle effect, a generational effect, a historical effect, or some combination of all three. It may be that people simply become less tolerant as they grow older, perhaps through continual refine-ment of their beliefs, or experience with political misdeeds, or just because they get more set in their ways. But the differences we see may also be due to the cultural changes that have taken place between the years when the Elders grew up and formed their basic political outlook, and the days when the Xers did the same. Growing up in the forties and fifties was a very different experience from growing up in the seventies and eighties. Some have suggested that there has been a sustained and progressive cultural and value shift going on in Canada, that would help explain the laid-back Xer tendencies.[4] Since our study is only a single snapshot, we can't resolve this question for now—we would need to conduct the same survey a number of times over many years to track how attitudes change.

The one exception to the trend of youthful tolerance had to do with perks—and small, common perks at that. This reinforces the notion that in general resentment or envy of gains that are available only to others is important in shaping how they are viewed. Age here shows up as less experience in the workplace, and a lower position on the career ladder. Perks and gains—even those that can be justified economically—are so very close to blatant preferential treatment that it is hard for people not to resent those who receive them.

WHAT POLITICIANS NEED TO HEAR

When Canadians speak out on ethics, now and in the future, elected officials need to listen. They need to hear the fundamental ethical standards they will be expected to uphold. No matter how many extra complications and qualifications that political life and responsibilities introduce, a politician is still responsible to the citizens for his or her behaviour. If the rest of the House approves, that's nice, but if the voters aren't convinced, both the politician and the institutions of politics suffer. Politicians need to hear that the public is paying attention, perhaps not always as closely as the media and political scientists; but the public can have a long memory, and even after apparent abuses like the parliamentary pension scheme are corrected, they are remembered for a long time. Politicians need to hear that some Canadians are more tolerant than others, but this is no opportunity for targeted misbehaviour. Older Canadians are the harshest critics of politics and probably blame what they consider a decline in standards among the young on the very public failures of politicians.

And if it is too difficult to remember the totality of public opinion, then perhaps there are a few simple principles that can be kept in mind, words of advice from the Canadian public to those they elevate to office. They don't provide explicit guidance for particular situations, any more than the Golden Rule tells you how to deal with your neighbour's barking dog. Nor are they fool-proof, but they ought to keep the careful ones out of too much trouble.

RULES TO RULE BY: ADVICE FOR ELECTED OFFICIALS FROM CANADIANS

- Don't worry so much about your private lives: we are more understanding than you have been led to believe as long as you play straight with us in your official capacity. Keep your friends, but keep them out of the public purse.
- You may not be paid as much, but your image problem is worse than that of the most pampered celebrity, the most prima-donna pro athlete. Don't dare whine about how rough it is in public life, even if it is true. Suck it up, do your jobs, and be very careful about how you spend our money.
- Each of you is still one of us—never forget that you once were, and are destined to be again, a private citizen. The fact that you have a special job for a while doesn't make you a special person. If you start to think it does, you'd better believe we'll let you know.
- Listen to *us*, not the media—they didn't hire you, and we didn't elect them to represent our views. Strange as it may seem, we sometimes even prefer you to them. Speak *through* the media, not just *to* the media.
- It's time to stop waffling on conflict of interest. We don't have the answers, but we expect you to try to find them. Take the initiative and show us that you're big enough to admit you need guidance. We might just appreciate the candour.

- Never make a promise you won't, can't, shouldn't, or even might not be able to keep. Nothing is more damaging to your reputation—you end up either a liar or a fool. Really, we expect some of both, but try not to do it so blatantly.

It's really not all that much to ask, is it? At least it's worth a try—it would certainly be difficult for you to make things worse. . . .

Canada is not yet facing a true crisis of legitimacy: widespread insurrection and revolution are not afoot across the country. But public confidence in our leaders, and through them in our democracy as a system, is sagging. To a worrisome extent, the foundations have been weakened by neglect and continued lapses in ethical judgement. Eventually something has to give, and we should all prefer that it be the politicians rather than the political structures. A few wise decisions and some difficult but important commitments can reverse this trend. A simple public relations campaign can only smooth over a few irregularities in a pockmarked political landscape. What we need to do is improve actual relations between politicians and the public and strengthen the ties that bind citizens to their elected leaders. This book has attempted to draw a more detailed and specific ethical map of the country. Politicians need to pay more attention to their ethical compass, and using this map they can help steer Canada back on course.

A p p e n d i x

The
Research
Instrument

Political Ethics In Canada

Hello, my name is _____. I'm calling for a research project by five Canadian universities [*If respondent asks, the Universities are Guelph, Toronto, Montreal, York, and McMaster*]. We are doing a study of people's opinions about what politicians should or should not do. And we'd really like your help.

Can I speak to someone 18 years of age or older? Actually, I need to speak with the person who's had the most recent birthday.

[*Pause—get person—repeat first paragraph of opening if birthday person is not the one who first answered the phone*]

Your answers will be completely confidential. Have you got a few minutes? [*If respondent asks how long survey will take, say:* Actually, the whole survey will take about 20 minutes. Most people really enjoy it, so sometimes it may go a bit longer.]

[*If respondent asks about confidentiality or why he or she was picked*] Your phone number was chosen at random by a computer; we don't know your name, and all responses will be confidential. We would just like to ask you about your views.

Here's the first question:

1. Among the following five values, which is, for you personally, the
    most important of all?

equality	1		
compassion	2		
honesty	3		
freedom	4	*don't know*	6
tolerance	5	*refused*	7

2. And which is the second most important?

equality	1		
compassion	2		
honesty	3		
freedom	4	*don't know*	6
tolerance	5	*refused*	7

3. Generally speaking, would you say that most people can be trusted,
    or that you can't be too careful in dealing with people?

can be trusted	1	*don't know*	3
can't be too careful	2	*refused*	4

4. Here is a list of different institutions. For each one, can you tell me
    how much confidence you have in them: A great deal, some, a
    little or none at all. (**Circle their response**).

		A Great Deal	Some	A Little	None at all	*Don't Know*	*Refused*
a.	The Courts	1	2	3	4	5	6
b.	The Media	1	2	3	4	5	6
c.	Parliament	1	2	3	4	5	6
d.	Civil Service	1	2	3	4	5	6
e.	The Senate	1	2	3	4	5	6

5. Here is a list of groups of people. I'd like you to tell me if you think the ethical principles of these people **ARE** higher, lower, or about the same as those of the average person:

		Higher	Lower	About Same	Don't Know	Refused
a.	Judges	1	2	3	4	5
b.	Journalists	1	2	3	4	5
c.	Members of Parliament	1	2	3	4	5
d.	Civil Servants	1	2	3	4	5

6. Here's a list of things that some people do. We are interested in whether you think each one is acceptable or unacceptable [*read item a.*]

		Usually Acceptable	Sometimes Acceptable	Rarely Acceptable	Never Acceptable	Don't Know	Refused
a.	Failing to report damage accidentally done to a parked car	1	2	3	4	5	6

Is that: **usually acceptable, sometimes acceptable, rarely acceptable, or never acceptable?** [*circle response above*]

		Usually Acceptable	Sometimes Acceptable	Rarely Acceptable	Never Acceptable	Don't Know	Refused
b.	Paying cash to a plumber to avoid taxes	1	2	3	4	5	6
c.	Lying to protect a friend	1	2	3	4	5	6
d.	Accepting a gift for doing your job	1	2	3	4	5	6
e.	Not telling the whole truth to avoid embarrassment	1	2	3	4	5	6
f.	Claiming benefits which you are not entitled to	1	2	3	4	5	6

		Usually Acceptable	Sometimes Acceptable	Rarely Acceptable	Never Acceptable	Don't Know	Refused
g.	Using your influence to get a friend a job	1	2	3	4	5	6
h.	Giving a police officer money to avoid a speeding ticket	1	2	3	4	5	6
i.	Not declaring to customs things brought in from another country	1	2	3	4	5	6
j.	Breaking a promise	1	2	3	4	5	6

Now here are some different situations. We're going to use a scale that goes from 0 to 10, 0 means **totally unacceptable**, and 10 means **totally acceptable**. Choose the number from 0 to 10 that best reflects **your** view. Here's the first situation: (*Circle the appropriate numerical response*)

7. A Cabinet Minister is seeing a psychiatrist and decides not to tell the Prime Minister about it.

   0 1 2 3 4 5 6 7 8 9 10   *don't know* **(11)**   *refused* **(12)**

Remember, we're using numbers: 0 means **totally unacceptable** and 10 means **totally acceptable**. You can choose **any** number between 0 and 10.

8. An MP who has cancer, denies this fact when asked by a journalist.

   0 1 2 3 4 5 6 7 8 9 10   *don't know* **(11)**   *refused* **(12)**

9. The Prime Minister appoints a loyal party supporter to head the CBC

   0 1 2 3 4 5 6 7 8 9 10   *don't know* **(11)**   *refused* **(12)**

10. Do you think people in politics make these sorts of appointments frequently (*yes or no*)?

   yes (1)   **no (2)**   *don't know* **(3)**   *refused* **(4)**

[*If necessary, repeat instructions on using scale*]

11. A campaign worker is rewarded with a government job, for which he is fully qualified.

    0 1 2 3 4 5 6 7 8 9 10 *don't know* (11) *refused* (12)

12. At Christmas a Member of Parliament accepts a bottle of wine from a constituent who is grateful for help in speeding up the paperwork to get a passport.

    0 1 2 3 4 5 6 7 8 9 10 *don't know* (11) *refused* (12)

13. Do you think people in politics frequently accept gifts like this (*yes or no*)?

    yes (1)   **no** (2)   *don't know* (3)   *refused* (4)

14. On a trip to the North-West Territories, a Cabinet Minister meets with a group of local artists who present him with a valuable carving. On his return, he displays the carving in his home.

    0 1 2 3 4 5 6 7 8 9 10 *don't know* (11) *refused* (12)

15. An MP owns a local clothing store. He votes in favour of legislation to provide loans to small business.

    0 1 2 3 4 5 6 7 8 9 10 *don't know* (11) *refused* (12)

16. Do you think people in politics do this sort of thing frequently (*yes or no*)?

    yes (1)   **no** (2)   *don't know* (3)   *refused* (4)

    [*If necessary, repeat instructions on using scale*]

17. The Minister of Tourism owns a large hotel.

    0 1 2 3 4 5 6 7 8 9 10 *don't know* (11) *refused* (12)

18. The Minister of Agriculture owns a large farm.

    0 1 2 3 4 5 6 7 8 9 10 *don't know* (11) *refused* (12)

19. A Cabinet Minister helps a builder get an important government contract. In return, the Minister accepts the free use of the builder's cottage for a week.

    0 1 2 3 4 5 6 7 8 9 10   *don't know* (11)   *refused* (12)

20. Do you think people in politics do this sort of thing frequently (*yes or no*)?

    yes (1)   **no (2)**   *don't know* (3)   *refused* (4)

21. A Senator who has no other outside employment, agrees to serve as a corporate director for a small fee.

    0 1 2 3 4 5 6 7 8 9 10   *don't know* (11)   *refused* (12)

22. An MP uses the parliamentary restaurant, where the prices are subsidized, to host dinners for visiting constituents.

    0 1 2 3 4 5 6 7 8 9 10   *don't know* (11)   *refused* (12)

23. Do you think people in politics do this sort of thing frequently (*yes or no*)?

    yes (1)   **no (2)**   *don't know* (3)   *refused* (4)

24. After working late on constituency business, an MP takes a cab home and charges it to the government.

    0 1 2 3 4 5 6 7 8 9 10   *don't know* (11)   *refused* (12)

25. During an election campaign, a political party promises not to close any hospitals. After the election, the party finds it must close one hospital because of its deficit-reduction plan.

    0 1 2 3 4 5 6 7 8 9 10   *don't know* (11)   *refused* (12)

26.   Do you think people in politics do this sort of thing frequently (*yes or no*)?

   yes (1)   **no (2)**   *don't know* **(3)**   *refused* **(4)**

27.   A Cabinet Minister learns that his deputy minister is being secretly investigated by the RCMP. To protect the reputation of his deputy, the Minister claims to know nothing about the investigation when asked in Parliament.

   0 1 2 3 4 5 6 7 8 9 10   *don't know* (11)   *refused* (12)

For the next few examples, I'd like you to tell me what **you** think the politician should do. Here is the first situation:

28.   A Cabinet Minister is seeing a marriage counselor. A journalist asks him if this is true. Should the Minister say:

   (a) "It's none of your business"
   (b) "Every marriage has its rough spots"   (d) *don't know*
   (c) "Yes, I'm seeing a counselor"   (e) *refused*

29.   Do you think that, given this situation, most people in politics would choose the same answer as you (*yes or no*)?

   yes (1)   **no (2)**   *don't know* **(3)**   *refused* **(4)**

30.   The Minister of Justice has to appoint a judge. Who should the Minister consider:

   (a) Any qualified persons
   (b) Qualified persons who are
        loyal party members
   (c) Qualified persons selected   (d) *don't know*
        by a non-partisan committee   (e) *refused*

31. Do you think that, given this situation, most people in politics would choose the same answer as you (*yes or no*)?

    yes (1)   **no (2)**   *don't know* **(3)**   *refused* **(4)**

32. An MP helps a local restaurant owner get a liquor license. A few weeks later, the owner sends the MP a cheque for $5,000. The MP should:

    (a) return the cheque
    (b) cash the cheque and
         donate the money to charity   (d) *don't know*
    (c) report the matter to the police   (e) *refused*

33. Do you think that, given this situation, most people in politics would choose the same answer as you (*yes or no*)?

    yes (1)   **no (2)**   *don't know* **(3)**   *refused* **(4)**

34. The former Energy Minister is asked by his brother, who works for an oil company, for advice as to who to talk to about a tax break for his company. The former Minister should:

    (a) be as helpful as possible
    (b) refer his brother to an industry
         consultant
    (c) say he's sorry, but he can't   (d) *don't know*
         give any advice   (e) *refused*

    [*If the respondent inquires about when the Minister resigned, the answer is "6 months ago."*]

35. Do you think that, given this situation, most people in politics would choose the same answer as you (*yes or no*)?

    yes (1)   **no (2)**   *don't know* **(3)**   *refused* **(4)**

36. A Cabinet Minister is faced with a large debt following his reelection. His advisers tell him that the best way to raise money is to invite people to a private breakfast meeting where anyone who pays $500 can talk to the Minister about their concerns. Should the Minister:

    (a) go along with the plan
    (b) set no fee, but encourage
        people to make donations   (d) *don't know*
    (c) reject the idea   (e) *refused*

37. Do you think that, given this situation, most people in politics would choose the same answer as you (*yes or no*)?

    yes (1)   **no (2)**   *don't know* **(3)**   *refused* **(4)**

38. A Minister has to attend an important meeting in Europe. He is issued a first-class plane ticket. His wife, who sees very little of her husband, would like to go along. Should the Minister:

    (a) bring his wife along at his own expense
    (b) trade in his first class fare for
        two seats in economy   (d) *don't know*
    (c) go alone   (e) *refused*

39. Do you think that, given this situation, most people in politics would choose the same answer as you (*yes or no*)?

    yes (1)   **no (2)**   *don't know* **(3)**   *refused* **(4)**

40. The Minister of Finance is scheduled to make a major speech to international investors about the Canadian economy. At the last minute he learns that the deficit is much larger than expected. Should the Minister:

    (a) present the new deficit estimates
    (b) cancel his speech
    (c) make the speech, and say nothing   (d) *don't know*
        about the deficit   (e) *refused*

41. Do you think that, given this situation, most people in politics would choose the same answer as you (*yes or no*)?

yes (1)   no (2)   *don't know* **(3)**   *refused* **(4)**

Now I am going to read you some statements. I'd like you to tell me if you **strongly agree, somewhat agree, somewhat disagree,** or **strongly disagree. (Circle responses).**

	Strongly Agree	Somewhat Agree	Somewhat Disagree	Strongly Disagree	Don't Know	Refused
42. No matter what we do, we can never put an end to political corruption in this country.	1	2	3	4	5	6
43. Politicians cannot expect to have the same degree of privacy as everyone else.	1	2	3	4	5	6
44. Political corruption is a widespread problem in this country.	1	2	3	4	5	6
45. Obedience and respect for authority are the most important virtues children should learn.	1	2	3	4	5	6
46. People who run for election are usually out for themselves.	1	2	3	4	5	6
47. The media say too much about the private lives of politicians.	1	2	3	4	5	6

	Strongly Agree	Somewhat Agree	Somewhat Disagree	Strongly Disagree	Don't Know	Refused
48. We should not expect MPs to have higher ethical standards than the average person.	1	2	3	4	5	6
49. Journalists judge politicians by standards that journalists themselves don't meet.	1	2	3	4	5	6
50. What cabinet ministers do in their private lives tells us whether they would be good leaders.	1	2	3	4	5	6
51. People distrust politicians because they don't understand what politics is all about.	1	2	3	4	5	6
52. In general, politicians are very well-paid.	1	2	3	4	5	6
53. It is important to protect fully the rights of radicals.	1	2	3	4	5	6
54. Loyalty to friends is often more important than obeying the law.	1	2	3	4	5	6
55. No MP should be allowed to hold office for more than 10 years.	1	2	3	4	5	6

Now let's think about some comparisons:

56. Do you think there is **more, less,** or **the same** amount of corruption in government as there is in business?

more (1)   **less (2)**   **same (3)**   *don't know* **(4)**   *refused* **(5)**

57. Do you think women politicians have **higher, lower,** or **about the same** ethical standards as male politicians?

higher (1)   **lower (2)**   **same (3)**   *don't know* **(4)**   *refused* **(5)**

Some think that corruption is part of politics, and that there is nothing we can do about it. Others think it is possible to reduce it if we take the proper steps. Do you think the following proposals would reduce corruption **a lot, a little,** or **not at all?**

		A lot	A little	Not at all	Don't Know	Refused
58.	Bring in stiffer penalties for corrupt behaviour.	1	2	3	4	5
59.	Require all politicians to reveal publicly their tax returns.	1	2	3	4	5
60.	Make politicians take a course on public ethics.	1	2	3	4	5
61.	Create an independent ethics commission to investigate the public's complaints.	1	2	3	4	5
62.	Screen those seeking public office for gaps in their personal ethics.	1	2	3	4	5

63. Is there anything else that you think could be done to improve standards in government?

_____

_____

_____

_____

_____

Finally, would you mind telling me a few things about yourself. [*Circle response, or fill in as required*]

64. In what year were you born?   _____
    [*if respondent gives age instead, record it here*]

don't know	1
refused	2

65. And, were you born in Canada?

yes	1	*don't know*	3
no	2	*refused*	4

66. What is the highest level of schooling you've completed? I'll read out categories and you can stop me at the one that applies to you. [*If you are not sure which category respondent's answer goes in, **write down** their answer*]

Elementary	1		
Some High School	2		
High School graduate	3		
Some Technical or College education	4		
Completed Technical or College	5		
Some University	6		
Completed B.A.	7		
Completed M.A.	8		
Completed Ph.D.	9		
Medicine	10	*don't know*	12
Law	11	*refused*	13

67. What is your religious affiliation? Is it:

Protestant   1
Catholic   2
Jewish   3
Another religion   4   don't know   6
none   5   refused   7

[If respondent chooses 'none' or refuses, skip to question 69]

68. How often do you attend your place of worship? [read categories]

more than once a week   1
once a week   2
once a month   3
just a few times a year 4   don't know   6
never   5   refused   7

69. How important is Religion in your life? [read categories]

very important   1
somewhat important   2
a little important   3   don't know   6
not at all important 4   refused   7

70. What is the first language you learned and still understand?

English   1
French   2   don't know   4
Other   3   refused   5

71. Could you please tell me about your **total** household income—we don't need the exact amount. I'll read out some categories—just tell me which one applies to your household.

under $20,000   1
20–40,000   2
40–60,000   3
60–80,000   4   don't know   6
over 80,000   5   refused   7

72.   Are you presently working for pay?

yes	1	*don't know*	3
no	2	*refused*	4

73.   [*If respondent says '***no***', ask*] Are you:

unemployed	1		
a homemaker	2		
retired	3		
a student	4	*don't know*	6
something else	5	*refused*	7

74.   What is the occupation of the main income earner in your household?

_____	*don't know*	1
	refused	2

75.   In general, would you say you are very **interested, fairly interested, not very interested,** or **not interested at all in politics?**

very interested	1		
fairly interested	2		
not very interested	3	*don't know*	5
not interested at all	4	*refused*	6

76.   We would now like to know how well some political figures are known. Do you happen to remember the name of:

	Correct	Incorrect	Don't Know	Refused
a. The Prime Minister of Canada	1	2	3	4
b. The Premier of your Province	1	2	3	4
c. The President of the United States	1	2	3	4
d. The Federal Minister of Finance	1	2	3	4

77. If a federal election were held today which party would you vote
    for? [Do **NOT** read out party names]

PC	1		
Liberal	2		
NDP	3		
Reform	4		
Bloc Quebecois	5		
Other	6	don't know	8
None	7	refused	9

78. And if a provincial election were held today which party would
    you vote for? [write in party name]

_____	don't know 1
	refused 2

79. Would you say you live in:

a big city	1		
a suburb	2		
a small town	3	don't know	5
a rural area [includes a village]	4	refused	6

80. Have you ever talked to a federal or provincial politician?

yes	1	don't know	3
no	2	refused	4

[Do NOT ask following questions, simply record info on form]

81. Is respondent: Male 1   Female 2

82. Which province is the respondent living in? Province Name (area code):

    _____   _____

Thank you for your time and views. We appreciate your comments and assistance.

If respondent asks how they might receive a copy of the results of the study, tell them they can write to the Political Ethics Group, The Department of Political Studies, University of Guelph, N1G 2W1.

→ Notes

Introduction

1. For a discussion of drops in traditional forms of participation and rises in alternative forms, see Neil Nevitte, *The Decline of Deference: Canadian Value Change in Cross-National Perspective* (Toronto: Broadview, 1996).
2. United Nations Development Programme (UNDP), *Human Development Report 1997* (New York: Oxford University Press, 1997), 204. According to the Human Development Index Ranking, Canada was ranked first in 1997, 1994, and 1992.
3. See also Figures 2.2 and 2.3.
4. A striking example from early 1998 was the continual climb in President Bill Clinton's approval ratings even as media pundits were predicting his imminent downfall over the Monica Lewinsky affair.

Chapter One

1. Edward Greenspon, 'Chrétien apologizes over GST promise', *The Globe and Mail*, 17 Dec. 1996, A1.
2. See André Blais, Richard Nadeau, Élisabeth Gidengil, and Neil Nevitte, *Campaign Dynamics in the 1997 Canadian Election* (Montreal: Typescript, 1998).
3. André Blais and Élisabeth Gidengil, *Representative Democracy: The Views of Canadians* (Ottawa: Royal Commission on Electoral Reform and Party Financing, 1992).
4. Colin Campbell and William Christian, *Parties, Leaders, and Ideologies in Canada* (Whitby, Ont.: McGraw-Hill Ryerson, 1996).
5. See Michael M. Atkinson, 'The Integrity Agenda: Lead Us Not into Temptation', in Susan Phillips, ed., *How Ottawa Spends: Mid-Life Crises* (Ottawa: Carleton University Press, 1995).
6. Ontario, Office of Commissioner on Conflict of Interest, *Annual Report 1990–1* (Toronto: 1992), 6–9.
7. Ian Greene, 'Conflict of Interest and the Canadian Constitution: An Analysis of Conflict of Interest Rules for Canadian Cabinet Ministers', *Canadian Journal of Political Science* 23: 2 (June 1990), 246.

8. *Report of the Task Force on Conflict of Interest* [Starr-Sharp Report] (Ottawa: Minister of Supply and Services, 1984).

9. Most provinces have cleared this hurdle and have actual conflict-of-interest legislation.

10. This British *Register of Members' Interests* is discussed thoroughly in Maureen Mancuso, *The Ethical World of British MPs* (Kingston: McGill-Queens University Press, 1995).

11. The spouses argued successfully that only the member, and not his or her family, ought to undergo the restrictions and scrutiny required of politicians. Since the spouses are not public officials themselves, they should not be subject to the same regulations.

12. In Mancuso's study of British MPs, those members identified as 'muddlers' certainly were grappling with their consciences and the system in an attempt to do the right thing. See Mancuso, *Ethical World*.

Chapter Two

1. And only free adult males qualified as citizens.

2. A discussion of how definitions emerge from an individual's social context can be found in Angela Gorta and Suzie Forell, 'Layers of Decision: Linking Social Definitions of Corruption and Willingness to Take Action', *Crime, Law and Social Change* 23 (1995), 315–43.

3. For a thorough overview of recent work in this field, see Kathryn L. Malec, 'Public Attitudes Towards Corruption: Twenty-Five Years of Research', in H. G. Frederickson, ed., *Ethics and Public Administration* (New York: M. E. Sharpe, 1993), 13–27.

4. Some good examples of elite attitudinal studies are Edmund Beard and Stephen Horn, *Congressonal Ethics: The View from the House* (Washington: Brookings, 1975); Susan Welch and John G. Peters, 'Attitudes of U.S. State Legislators Toward Political Corruption: Some Preliminary Findings', *Legislative Studies Quarterly* 2 (Nov. 1977): 445–63; Michael M. Atkinson and Maureen Mancuso, 'Do We Need a Code of Conduct for Politicians? The Search for an Elite Political Culture of Corruption in Canada', *Canadian Journal of Political Science* 18 (Sept. 1985): 459–80; and Maureen Mancuso, *The Ethical World of British MPs* (Kingston: McGill-Queens, 1995).

5. Previous mass studies include Michael Johnston, 'Right and Wrong in American Politics: Popular Conceptions of Corruption', *Polity* 18:

3 (1986), 367–91; D. Clarke, 'A Community Relations Approach to Corruption: The Case of Hong Kong', *Corruption and Reform* 2 (1987), 235–57; and Kenneth M. Gibbons, 'Variations in Attitudes toward Corruption in Canada', in Arnold J. Heidenheimer et al., eds, *Political Corruption: A Handbook* (New Brunswick, N.J.: Transaction Books, 1989), 763–80.

6. One recent mass-elite comparison is Michael Jackson and Rodney Smith, 'Inside Moves and Outside Views: An Australian Case Study of Elite and Public Perceptions of Political Corruption', *Governance* 9 (Jan. 1996), 23–42. This study, however, was based on a rather small sample.

7. The 'irrational public' school of thought includes Phillip Converse, who argued that many people actually hold no consistent opinion on numerous issues. See his influential article, 'The Nature of Belief Systems in Mass Publics', in David E. Apter, ed., *Ideology and Discontent* (New York: Free Press, 1965), 206–61.

8. See Samuel L. Popkin, *The Reasoning Voter: Communication and Persuasion in Presidential Campaigns* (Chicago: University of Chicago Press, 1991) and Benjamin I. Page and Robert Y. Shapiro, *The Rational Public: Fifty Years of Trends in Americans' Policy Preferences* (Chicago: University of Chicago Press, 1992).

9. Held at the Elora Mill Inn, Elora, Ontario, October 1992.

10. Students in the Department of Political Science at Guelph surveyed some 400 local respondents by telephone in winter 1993. Colleagues at Syracuse University conducted a parallel survey of 200 people in Onandaga County, New York. With some small adjustments for national differences (MP was replaced with member of Congress, for example), the questionnaires were the same.

11. For example, our original questions used both negative and positive numbers to indicate disagreement or agreement with a statement, or disapproval or approval of a situation. Over the phone, this often proved difficult to explain, and distracting to the respondents. For the final survey we used a more intuitive 'zero-to-ten' scale.

12. We are indebted to David Northup of the Institute for Social Research at York University for assistance in training our interviewers.

13. A 'stratified' sample is one that is specifically constructed to maintain the same distribution as the total population. A regionally

stratified sample thus has roughly the same proportion of Ontarians, westerners, and so on, as does the Canadian general public. Stratification helps prevent any regional biases that might creep into the survey.

14. In some cases, up to 10 callbacks were needed to schedule an interview time convenient for the respondent, or to discard a number as unreachable. Calls were placed at all times of the day (across the six time zones), and records were kept of the number of attempts and the response elicited: refusal, no answer, busy signal, answering machine, completed survey, or business (not a household).

15. Response rates for Ontario and Quebec were lower than in the other eight provinces.

16. Nevitte, *The Decline of Deference*.

17. The scale was repeated after the first scenario was presented and again after each item if this was deemed necessary. The respondents seemed to catch on, though, and were able to give a numerical response without the constant reminder of the scale.

18. One of the first studies to employ such a method was Edmund Beard and Stephen Horn, *Congressional Ethics: The View from the House* (Washington: Brookings, 1975).

19. The next major publication of our findings will explore our data in more detail and will cross-reference the results of the public survey with identical surveys of a sample of federal and provincial politicians, and with a sample of media representatives.

20. Technically, the terms for these varieties are measures of central tendency, variability, and correlation. A good introduction to statistics is Levin and Fox, *Elementary Statistics in Social Research*, 7th edn (New York: Longman, 1997).

21. In order to make it more confusing to outsiders, the standard way of expressing this degree of certainty is '$p < .05$', which means that the probability of being wrong is no more than 5 per cent (which is the same as a 95 per cent chance of being right). 99 per cent certainty would be expressed as '$p < .01$' The lower p is, the stronger the conclusion.

22. Statistics has several different kinds of ways to indicate an average, but the mean, which is the sum of scores divided by the number of scores, is the closest to the usual meaning of 'average'.

23. Carol Gilligan, *In a Different Voice* (Cambridge, Mass.: Harvard University Press, 1982); Roberta Siegel, *Ambition and Accommodation: How Women View Gender Relations* (Chicago: University of Chicago Press, 1996); John Gray, *Men Are from Mars, Women Are from Venus* (New York: Harper Collins, 1994).

24. Kathryn Malec provides a complete listing of these correlates in 'Public Attitudes Towards Corruption'.

25. For recent discussions of the particular challenges women face in the political realm, see Sylvia Bashevkin, *Women on the Defensive: Living through Conservative Times* (Chicago: University of Chicago Press, 1998) and Heather MacIvor, *Women and Politics in Canada* (Peterborough, Ont.: Broadview, 1996).

26. Atkinson and Mancuso, 'Do We Need a Code of Conduct?'

27. Our groups and the names for the groups are drawn from Michael Adams, *Sex in the Snow: Canadian Social Values at the End of the Millennium* (Toronto: Viking, 1997).

28. An explanation of factor analysis is beyond the scope of this book; see Paul Kline, *An Easy Guide to Factor Analysis* (New York: Routledge, 1994). The gist of the technique is that it identifies items that 'go together' and produces from a large number of separate questions a smaller number of underlying 'factors', which encapsulate the essence of how the questions were answered.

29. See Welch and Peters, 'Attitudes of U.S. State Legislators'.

Chapter Three

1. Ian Greene, 'Conflict of Interest and the Canadian Constitution: An Analysis of Conflict of Interest Rules for Canadian Cabinet Ministers', *Canadian Journal of Political Science* 23: 2 (June 1990), 233–56.

2. Andrew Stark, 'Beyond Quid pro Quo: What's Wrong with Private Gain from Public Office', *American Political Science Review* 91: 1 (March 1997), 108–20.

3. Ian Greene and David Shugarman, *Honest Politics* (Toronto: Lorimer, 1997), 80. See also Graham Leslie, *Breach of Promise: Sacred Ethics under Vander Zalm* (Madeira Park, B.C.: Harbour, 1991).

4. Quoted in Greene and Shugarman, *Honest Politics*, 82.

5. Commission of Inquiry into the Facts and Allegations of Conflict of Interest Concerning the Honourable Sinclair M. Stevens [Parker Commission] *Report* (Ottawa: Supply and Services, 1987), 29–30.

6. Parker Commission, *Report*, 329.

7. Privy Council Office, *Members of Parliament and Conflict of Interest* [MacEachen Green Paper] (Ottawa: Information Canada, 1973), 1.

8. Parker Commission, *Report*, 35.

9. Task Force on Conflict of Interest, *Report* [Starr-Sharp Report] (Ottawa: Supply and Services Canada, 1984), 29.

10. William Walker, 'Gigantes didn't talk of deal panel told', *Toronto Star*, 12 Aug. 1994.

11. Greene, 'Conflict of Interest'.

12. This question is difficult to answer definitively because the apparent qualifications for board and Senate membership are similar: successful and prominent businesspeople gravitate toward both CEOs are attracted by the same qualities that interest Prime Ministers. The important distinction is that Senate membership confers additional privileges and access to the machinery of government, if not actual power. For a more detailed discussion of these issues, see Colin Campbell, *The Canadian Senate: A Lobby from Within* (Toronto: Macmillan, 1978).

13. Michael Adams, *Sex in the Snow: Canadian Social Values at the End of the Millennium* (Toronto: Viking, 1997), 103.

14. Adams, *Sex in the Snow*, 60.

15. Gilligan, *In a Different Voice*.

16. Adams, *Sex in the Snow*, 155–6.

17. Blais et al., *Campaign Dynamics*.

Chapter Four

1. In *Conscience and Popularity*, Burke said: 'I wish to be a member of parliament, to have my share of doing good and resisting evil. It would therefore be absurd to renounce my objects, in order to obtain my seat.'

2. Robert Fife and John Warren, *A Capital Scandal* (Toronto: Key Porter, 1991).

3. Much of the outrage stemmed from allegations that the medical problems were conveniently exaggerated. Even so, any other Canadian unable to continue working due to illness would have to go on long-term disability. Certainly the pension benefits from a Senate seat are as generous as the salary. And by returning to Canada and his OHIP coverage, Thompson would have no worries about medical expenses. After much public outcry, his Senate colleagues finally voted to suspend him in February 1998; Thompson subsequently resigned his seat.

4. Before his Reform Party became the Official Opposition in 1997, Manning had proposed renting Stornoway out as a bingo hall, or selling it outright. Manning's predecessor as Leader of the Opposition, Lucien Bouchard, managed to resist the lure of Stornoway, although his objection was based on the separatist ideology of the Bloc Québécois, which would have made it politically dangerous to take up residence in a formal symbol of the country he wished to leave.

5. In 1998 it was recommended that the tax-free allowance be eliminated in exchange for a parliamentary pay increase. Since the increase would be taxed normally, the net result to MPs, as well as the public purse, would be zero. This troubling symbolism of a raise still makes it difficult to defend.

6. Fife and Warren, A Capital Scandal, 62–3.

7. See articles 'MP admits mistake in credit scandal: Ethel Blondin-Andrew says she routinely reimbursed the public treasury for private expenses', Vancouver Sun, 1 Nov. 1996, A2; and 'MP assailed for using government credit card to buy fur coat', Vancouver Sun, 29 Oct. 1996.

8. Dennis F. Thompson, 'Mediated Corruption: The Case of the Keating Five', American Political Science Review 87: 2 (June 1993), 369–77.

9. Doris Hilts, 'Took Gifts, Cabinet Ministers Tell Jury', The Globe and Mail, 8 Dec. 1982.

Chapter Five

1. Is it patronage if these supporters also have the necessary qualifications? Some say no. According to Colwell and Thomas, patronage

should be distinguished from 'political appointments' where there is some attention paid to qualifications and competence, not just political service. See Randy Colwell and Paul G. Thomas, 'Parliament and the Patronage Issue', *Journal of Canadian Studies* 22 (Summer 1987), 163. Unfortunately, not many appointments fall neatly into these two categories, and politicians are frequently given to defending patronage on the grounds that competent people shouldn't be disqualified from holding appointed office just because of their previous partisan attachments.

2. Frank Anechiarico and James B. Jacobs, *The Pursuit of Absolute Integrity* (Chicago: University of Chicago Press, 1996), chap. 2.
3. Jeffery Simpson, *Spoils of Power* (Toronto: Collins, 1988), 12.
4. Albert Breton, 'Patronage and Corruption in Hierarchies', *Journal of Canadian Studies* 22 (Summer 1987), 19–33; Vincent Lemieux, *Le patronage politique* (Quebec City: Presses Université Laval, 1977).
5. Reg Whitaker, 'Between Patronage and Bureaucracy: Democratic Politics in Transition', *Journal of Canadian Studies* 22 (Summer 1987), 55–71.
6. Both quotations are taken from Norman Ward, 'The Politics of Patronage: James Gardiner and Federal Appointments in the West, 1935–57', *Canadian Historical Review* 53 (Sept. 1977), 298.
7. Sharon Sutherland, 'The Canadian Federal Government: Patronage, Unity, Security, and Purity', in John W. Langford and Allan Tupper, eds., *Corruption, Character, and Conduct: Essays on Canadian Government Ethics* (Toronto: Oxford University Press, 1994), 121–2 and 113–50.
8. S.J.R. Noel, 'Dividing the Spoils: The Old and New Rules of Patronage in Canadian Politics', *Canadian Journal of Political Science* 22 (Summer 1987), 79–80.
9. Michael M. Atkinson, 'The Integrity Agenda: Lead Us Not into Temptation', in Susan Phillips, ed., *How Ottawa Spends: Mid-Life Crises* (Ottawa: Carleton University Press, 1995).
10. Samuel Huntington, 'Modernization and Corruption', in Arnold Heidenheimer, Michael Johnston, and Victor Levine, *Political Corruption: A Handbook* (New Brunswick, N.J.: Transaction Books, 1989).

11. John English, *The Decline of Politics: The Conservatives and the Party System, 1901–1920* (Toronto: University of Toronto Press, 1977).
12. Simpson, *Spoils of Power*, 362.
13. Claire Hoy, *Friends in High Places: Politics and Patronage in the Mulroney Government* (Toronto: Key Porter, 1987), chap. 14.
14. John Peters and Susan Welch, 'Political Corruption in America: A Search for Definitions and a Theory. Or If Political Corruption Is in the Mainstream of American Politics, Why Is It Not in the Mainstream of American Politics Research', *American Political Science Review* 74 (1980), 974–84. See also Vincent Lemieux and Raymond Hudon, *Patronage et politique au Québec* (Sillery, 1975).
15. Duff Spafford, 'Highway Employment and Provincial Elections', *Canadian Journal of Political Science* 14: 1 (Mar. 1981), 135–42.
16. Jacques Bourgault and Stéphane Dion, 'Public Sector Ethics in Quebec: The Contrasting Society', in Langford and Tupper, 83.

Chapter Six

1. Amy Gutmann and Dennis Thompson, eds, *Ethics and Politics: Cases and Comments* (Chicago: Nelson-Hall, 1990), 39.
2. Opposition critic Moe Sihota, quoted in Gillian Shaw, 'Allowed a Lie, Minister Tells Legislature', *Vancouver Sun*, 26 May 1989.
3. Harvey Simmons, 'Lying in High Places Threatens Democracy', *Toronto Star*, 29 Dec. 1991.
4. The *Globe and Mail* editorial writers weren't convinced. They argued, 'The government was elected on a promise in which it never believed. It promised to kill a tax for which it had no better alternative, knowing full well that every major study had shown there was no alternative.' *The Globe and Mail*, 25 Apr. 1996.
5. For a comprehensive look at political promises, see Anthony Hyde, *Promises, Promises: Breaking Faith in Canadian Politics* (Toronto: Viking, 1997).
6. André Pratte, *Le Syndrome de Pinocchio: Essai sur le mensonge en politique* (Montreal: Boréal, 1997).
7. 'Un jour à la fois', TVA, 17 Mar. 1997.
8. Pratte, *Le Syndrome de Pinocchio*, 133.
9. Dennis F. Thompson, *Political Ethics and Public Office* (Cambridge, Mass.: Harvard University Press, 1987).

10. For a discussion of this question see Sissela Bok, *Secrets: On the Ethics of Concealment and Revelation* (New York: Pantheon, 1982), 254–8.

11. David Vienneau, 'Politicians Defend Their Right to Privacy', *Toronto Star*, 18 Jan. 1988.

12. These relationships are particularly strong, exceeding the $p < .01$ level of confidence.

13. Bok, *Secrets*.

14. Paul Ekman, *Telling Lies: Clues to Deceit in the Marketplace, Politics, and Marriage* (New York: W.W. Norton, 1992), 27.

15. Again, this correlation exceeds the $p < .01$ level.

Conclusion

1. See Welch and Peters, 'Attitudes of U.S. State Legislators'; Atkinson and Mancuso, 'Do We Need a Code of Conduct?'; Mancuso, *The Ethical World of British MPs*.

2. Hyde, *Promises, Promises*.

3. Pratte, *Le Syndrome de Pinocchio*, 155.

4. Nevitte, *The Decline of Deference*.

→ Works Cited

Adams, Michael. *Sex in the Snow: Canadian Values at the End of the Millennium*. Toronto: Viking, 1997.

Anechiarico, Frank, and James B. Jacobs. *The Pursuit of Absolute Integrity*. Chicago: University of Chicago Press, 1996.

Atkinson, Michael M. 'The Integrity Agenda: Lead Us Not into Temptation'. In Susan Phillips, ed., *How Ottawa Spends: Mid-Life Crises*. Ottawa: Carleton University Press, 1995, 237–62.

Atkinson, Michael M., and Maureen Mancuso. 'Do We Need a Code of Conduct for Politicians? The Search for an Elite Political Culture of Corruption in Canada'. *Canadian Journal of Political Science* 18 (Sept. 1985), 459–80.

Bashevkin, Sylvia. *Women on the Defensive: Living Through Conservative Times*. Chicago: University of Chicago Press, 1998.

Beard, Edmund, and Stephen Horn. *Congressional Ethics: The View from the House*. Washington: Brookings, 1975.

Blais, André, and Elisabeth Gidengil. *Representative Democracy: The Views of Canadians*. Vol. 17 of the Research Studies of the Royal Commission on Electoral Reform and Party Financing. Ottawa: The Commission and Supply and Services Canada; Toronto: Dundurn Press.

Blais, André, Richard Nadeau, Elisabeth Gidengil, and Neil Nevitte. *Campaign Dynamics in the 1997 Canadian Election*. Montreal: Typescript, 1998.

Bok, Sissela. *Secrets: On the Ethics of Concealment and Revelation*. New York: Pantheon, 1982.

Bourgault, Jacques, and Stéphane Dion. 'Public Sector Ethics in Quebec: The Contrasting Society'. In John W. Langford and Allan Tupper, eds, *Corruption, Character and Conduct: Essays on Canadian Government Ethics*. Toronto: Oxford University Press, 1994, 67–89.

Breton, Albert. 'Patronage and Corruption in Hierarchies'. *Journal of Canadian Studies* 22 (Summer 1987), 19–33.

Burke, Edmund. *Conscience and Popularity*.

Campbell, Colin. *The Canadian Senate: A Lobby from Within*. Toronto: Macmillan, 1978.

Campbell, Colin, and William Christian. *Parties, Leaders, and Ideologies in Canada*. Whitby, Ont.: McGraw-Hill/Ryerson, 1996.

Canada. Commission of Inquiry into the Facts and Allegations of Conflict of Interest Concerning the Honourable Sinclair M. Stevens, *Report*. Ottawa: Supply and Services Canada, 1987.

Canada. Task Force on Conflict of Interest, *Report*. Ottawa: Supply and Services, 1984.

Clarke, David. 'A Community Relations Approach to Corruption: The Case of Hong Kong'. *Corruption and Reform* 2 (1987), 235–57.

Colwell, Randy, and Paul G. Thomas. 'Parliament and the Patronage Issue'. *Journal of Canadian Studies* 22: 2 (Summer 1987), 163–83.

Converse, Philip. 'The Nature of Belief Systems in Mass Publics'. In David E. Apter, ed., *Ideology and Discontent*. New York: Free Press, 1965, 206–61.

Ekman, Paul. *Telling Lies: Clues to Deceit in the Marketplace, Politics, and Marriage*. New York: Norton, 1992.

English, John. *The Decline of Politics: The Conservatives and the Party System, 1901–1920*. Toronto: University of Toronto Press, 1977.

Fife, Robert, and John Warren. *A Capital Scandal*. Toronto: Key Porter, 1991.

Gibbons, Kenneth M. 'Variations in Attitudes Toward Corruption in Canada'. In Arnold J. Heidenheimer, Michael Johnston, and Victor T. Levine, eds, *Political Corruption: A Handbook*. New Brunswick, N J : Transaction, 1989, 763–80.

Gilligan, Carol. *In a Different Voice*. Cambridge, Mass.: Harvard University Press, 1982.

Gorta, Angela, and Suzie Forell. 'Layers of Decision: Linking Social Definitions of Corruption and Willingness to Take Action'. *Crime, Law, and Social Change* 23 (1995), 315–43.

Gray, John. *Men Are from Mars, Women Are from Venus*. New York: Harper Collins, 1994.

Greene, Ian. 'Conflict of Interest and the Canadian Constitution: An Analysis of Conflict of Interest Rules for Canadian Cabinet Ministers'. *Canadian Journal of Political Science* 23: 2 (June 1990), 233–56.

Greene, Ian, and David Shugarman. *Honest Politics*. Toronto: Lorimer, 1997.

Greenspon, Edward. 'Chrétien Apologizes over GST Promise', *The Globe and Mail*, 17 Dec 1996, sec. A.

Gutman, Amy, and Dennis Thompson, eds. *Ethics and Politics: Cases and Comments*. Chicago: Nelson-Hall, 1990.

Hilts, Doris. 'Took Gifts, Cabinet Ministers Tell Jury'. *The Globe and Mail*, 8 Dec. 1982, sec. A.

Hoy, Claire. *Friends in High Places: Politics and Patronage in the Mulroney Government*. Toronto: Key Porter, 1987.

Huntington, Samuel. 'Modernization and Corruption'. In Arnold J. Heidenheimer, Michael Johnston, and Victor T. Levine, eds, *Political Corruption: A Handbook*. New Brunswick, N.J.: Transaction, 1989.

Hyde, Anthony. *Promises, Promises: Breaking Faith in Canadian Politics*. Toronto: Viking, 1997.

Jackson, Michael, and Rodney Smith. 'Inside Moves and Outside Views: An Australian Case Study of Elite and Public Perceptions of Political Corruption'. *Governance* 9 (Jan. 1996), 23–42.

Johnston, Michael. 'Right and Wrong in American Politics: Popular Conceptions of Corruption'. *Polity* 18: 3 (Spring 1986), 367–91.

Kline, Paul. *An Easy Guide to Factor Analysis*. New York: Routledge, 1994.

Lemieux, Vincent. *Le patronage politique: une étude comparative*. Quebec City: Presses Université Laval, 1977.

Lemieux, Vincent, and Raymond Hudon. *Patronage et politique au Québec*. Sillery, P.Q., 1975.

Leslie, Graham. *Breach of Promise: Socred Ethics Under Vander Zalm*. Madeira Park, B.C.: Harbour, 1991.

Levin, Jack, and James Alan Fox. *Elementary Statistics in Social Research*. 7th ed. New York: Longman, 1997.

McIlroy, Anne. 'Reformers Call P.M. a Liar, Hurl Liberal Handbook on Floor', *The Globe and Mail*, 25 Apr. 1996, sec. A.

MacIvor, Heather. *Women and Politics in Canada*. Peterborough, Ont.: Broadview, 1996.

Malec, Kathryn L. 'Public Attitudes Towards Corruption: Twenty-Five Years of Research'. In H.G. Frederickson, ed., *Ethics and Public Administration*. New York: M.E. Sharpe, 1993, 13–27.

Mancuso, Maureen. *The Ethical World of British MPs*. Kingston: McGill-Queens University Press, 1995.

'MP Admits Mistake in Credit Scandal: Ethel Blondin-Andrew Says She Routinely Reimbursed the Public Treasury for Private Expenses'. (Vancouver) *Sun*, 1 Nov. 1996, sec. A.

'MP Assailed for Using Government Credit Card to Buy Fur Coat'. (Vancouver) *Sun*. 29 Oct. 1996, sec. A.

Nevitte, Neil. *The Decline of Deference: Canadian Value Change in Cross-National Perspective.* Toronto: Broadview Press, 1996.

Noel, S.J.R. 'Dividing the Spoils: The Old and New Rules of Patronage in Canadian Politics'. *Journal of Canadian Studies* 22: 2 (Summer 1987), 72–95.

Ontario. Office of Commissioner on Conflict of Interest. *Annual Report.* 1990–91.

Page, Benjamin I., and Robert Y. Shapiro. *The Rational Public: Fifty Years of Trends in Americans' Policy Preferences.* Chicago: University of Chicago Press, 1992.

Parker Commission. *See* Canada. *Commission of Inquiry.* . . .

Peters, John, and Susan Welch. 'Political Corruption in America: A Search for Definitions and a Theory. Or If Political Corruption is in the Mainstream of American Politics, Why Is It Not in the Mainstream of American Politics Research'. *American Political Science Review* 72 (1980), 974–84.

Popkin, Samuel L. *The Reasoning Voter: Communication and Persuasion in Presidential Campaigns.* Chicago: University of Chicago Press, 1991.

Pratte, André. *Le Syndrome de Pinocchio: essai sur le mensonge en politique.* Montreal: Boréal, 1997.

Privy Council Office. *Members of Parliament and Conflict of Interest.* [MacEachen Green Paper] Ottawa: Information Canada, 1973.

Shaw, Gillian. 'Allowed a Lie, Minister Tells Legislature'. (Vancouver) *Sun*, 26 May 1989.

Siegel, Roberta. *Ambition and Accommodation: How Women View Gender Relations.* Chicago: University of Chicago Press, 1996.

Simmons, Harvey. 'Lying in High Places Threatens Democracy'. *Toronto Star.* 29 Dec. 1991.

Simpson, Jeffrey. *Spoils of Power.* Toronto: Collins, 1988.

Spafford, Duff. 'Highway Employment and Provincial Elections'. *Canadian Journal of Political Science* 14: 1 (Mar. 1981), 135–42.

Stark, Andrew. 'Beyond Quid Pro Quo: What's Wrong with Private Gain from Public Office'. *American Political Science Review* 91: 1 (Mar. 1997), 108–20.

Sutherland, Sharon. 'The Canadian Federal Government: Patronage, Unity, Security, and Purity'. In John W. Langford and Allan Tupper, eds,. *Corruption, Character and Conduct: Essays on Canadian Government Ethics*. Toronto: Oxford University Press, 1994, 113–50.

Thompson, Dennis F. *Political Ethics and Public Office*. Cambridge, Mass.: Harvard University Press, 1987.

————. 'Mediated Corruption: The Case of the Keating Five'. *American Political Science Review* 87: 2 (June 1993), 369–77.

United Nations Development Programme (UNDP). *Human Development Report*. New York: Oxford University Press, 1997.

'Un jour à la fois'. TVA. 17 Mar. 1997.

Vienneau, David. 'Politicians Defend Their Right to Privacy'. *Toronto Star*, 18 Jan. 1988, sec. A.

Walker, William. 'Gigantes Didn't Talk of Deal Panel Told'. *Toronto Star*, 12 Aug. 1994, sec. A.

Ward, Norman. 'The Politics of Patronage: James Gardiner and Federal Appointments in the West, 1935–57'. *Canadian Historical Review* 58: 3 (Sept. 1977), 294–310.

Welch, Susan, and John G. Peters. 'Attitudes of U.S. State Legislators Toward Political Corruption: Some Preliminary Findings'. *Legislative Studies Quarterly* 2 (Nov. 1977), 445–63.

Whitaker, Reg. 'Between Patronage and Bureaucracy: Democratic Politics in Transition'. *Journal of Canadian Studies* 22 (Summer 1987), 55–71.

→ Index